What makes you happy?

Fiona Robards is a psychologist with four Masters degrees — in Psychology, Art Therapy, Management and Public Health — who teaches Medical and Public Health students at the University of Sydney and UNSW Medical Schools. She regularly presents at conferences and contributes to a wide range of academic publications. Passionate about solution-focused approaches, Fiona researched *What Makes You Happy?* over a period of five years, synthesising ideas from her studies, counselling and management practice. You can follow Fiona on Twitter @whtmakesuhappy.

What makes you happy?

How small changes can lead to big improvements in your life

FIONA ROBARDS

EXISLE
PUBLISHING

First published 2014

Exisle Publishing Pty Ltd
'Moonrising', Narone Creek Road, Wollombi, NSW 2325, Australia
P.O. Box 60–490, Titirangi, Auckland 0642, New Zealand
www.exislepublishing.com

A CiP record for this book is available from the National Library of
Australia

ISBN 978 1 921966 31 6

Design and typesetting by Big Cat Design
Typeset in Minion Pro regular
Printed in Shenzhen, China, by Ink Asia

This book uses paper sourced under ISO 14001 guidelines from
well-managed forests and other controlled sources.

10 9 8 7 6 5 4 3 2 1

Disclaimer
While this book is intended as a general information resource and
all care has been taken in compiling the contents, this book does not
take account of individual circumstances and is not a substitute for
professional advice. Neither the author nor the publisher and their
distributors can be held responsible for any loss, claim or action that
may arise from reliance on the information contained in this book.

*To all people looking for simple
solutions to everyday happiness — for yourself,
for others and the environment*

CONTENTS

What makes you happy?

*Sometimes the questions are complicated
and the answers are simple.* Dr Seuss

What do you want most in life? Most people would answer, 'I just want to be happy.' Sounds simple, but what does happiness look like? And is the life you now lead bringing you closer to happiness?

To find out what makes you happy, let's break the complicated question into manageable pieces: What are you passionate about? What helps you to maintain a sense of hope and optimism? What rejuvenates you? Answering questions like these will help you to consciously create a life you really want to live, rather than one that just happens by chance or is based on things you don't truly value.

Another way of thinking about what makes you happy is to pinpoint those things that add to your wellbeing and quality of life. Wellbeing is about moving beyond 'just getting by' — it's about thriving and flourishing. But how do you get from one place to the other? Where's the map for the journey to happiness?

Creating happiness doesn't have to be an overwhelming task. While some people may need to make big changes to create a healthier lifestyle or stress less, setting goals to be happier need not include climbing mountains (although along the way, you might find you enjoy mountain climbing!).

The good news is that many simple, positive, healthy choices and activities promote wellbeing. Some people find that taking the time to experience simple pleasures

— patting a dog, reading to a child, cooking — brings great peace and enjoyment. For others, greater happiness involves simplifying their life: de-cluttering their home, developing healthy routines, making time to relax, and spending time with loved ones bring a sense of happiness that was missing.

Although each of us finds happiness in different ways and in different places, there are things we have in common: meaningful experiences, connections with friends and family, and practising gratitude and compassion bring value to our lives and increase our wellbeing and happiness.

If it's that simple, why aren't we happy yet? Many of us have adopted lifestyles that don't support happiness. We lead lives that are too rushed, too stressed and too focused on things that don't really matter. Our obsession with economic development is destroying the natural environment. And gaps between the haves and the have-nots are widening. We need to rethink our way of life because our unhealthy lifestyles are making us physically and mentally unwell. They're making us unhappier, not happier.

The solutions — doing things that support our wellbeing, finding opportunities to connect with others, and supporting the environment we live in — are intrinsically linked.

In your heart and mind you have very personal reasons for wanting to bring more happiness into your life. You might want to feel better in yourself or more optimistic and hopeful about the future. Perhaps you'd like to have a better appreciation of your skills, strengths and abilities. Or maybe you'd just like to find ways to stress less and simplify your life.

If we focus on the things that promote wellbeing for us, for others and the environment, we can stress less and live a calmer, happier life.

A path of possibilities

This book isn't just about a spring-clean for your life; it's also about starting a journey to sustainable, long-term wellbeing. A quick tidy-up never goes astray, but the key to real wellbeing is an everyday lifestyle filled with things that enhance happiness, such as caring for yourself and others.

My hope is that you will use this book to help you create extra happiness in your own time and on your own terms. It can help you to find space for extra happiness and explore the possibilities for bringing about positive change in your life. It will also help you appreciate what's already going well for you.

The ideas, information and activities in this book are designed to help you develop a vision of the life you want to lead. They will help you focus on your potential and the steps you need to take to make your vision a reality. Along the way, you'll see yourself in the context of your relationships, your community and the environment. See this book as a guide to help you be the best you can be, to allow new possibilities to emerge and blossom, and to make a contribution to improving the world around you.

There are questions throughout the book to help you develop your vision of a happier life. They are part of a solution-focused approach to counselling developed by Steve de Shazer and Insoo Kim Berg in the 1980s. Solution-focused approaches help people create changes that will bring greater contentment and happiness to their lives.

The solution-focused approach to achieving happiness in your life is simple, though not always easy. It looks like this:

1. *Develop a vivid, richly detailed picture of what happiness will look like in your life.*

2. *Think about what you do in your life and:*
   i *If it works, don't fix it*
   ii *If it works, do more of it*
   iii *If it doesn't work, do something different.*

3. *Give yourself a pat on the back for the things you already do that make you happy, and keep taking small steps to expand your happiness even more.*

Just as every person is different, so too is each person's pathway to happiness. In this book, rather than one-size-fits-all answers, you will find a range of questions and options to choose from. This gives you a real chance to explore what is right for *you*. This book does not tell you what to do or how to live your life; it provides you with a structure for planning and personal decision-making. You are developing your path of possibilities towards a unique, thoughtful, balanced and happy life. Ultimately, what makes you happy will be up to you: no one else can define happiness for you.

In Part 1 of this book, we start the journey by looking at your hopes and dreams, and the resources and plans you carry with you into each of the major areas of your life — your *life domains*. Thinking about our lives as having domains is a great way to help us zoom in on one aspect of life at a time, while remembering that all the domains are interrelated.

On this path, we are going to capture the best bits from the past and begin to create a vision of a brighter future. Let's start on the right foot by thinking about a few questions:

When you have achieved all you want from this journey, what might be different?

How can this difference be of benefit to you? How might it increase your happiness?

When there is more happiness in your life, what will you be doing differently that others might notice?

In Part 2, we delve into the ten primary domains of your life. In each domain you'll wander through questions to help you clarify ways you can stress less and simplify your life, and focus on positive and achievable things you can do today. As you move through each life domain, you have the chance to turn inspiration into action with a clear plan. At the end of each domain, you will find a commitment contract, which is an agreement with yourself. The contract helps you turn vague, fuzzy ideas into specific goals with strategies to bring them to life.

The last part of this book will help you develop plans to stay focused on your happiness. Planning for the changes you want to see will help you sustain progress and manage slip-ups. You might like to refer to this section as you make your way through the domains, especially if you meet challenges and obstacles on your path to change. This section also includes a 'big picture' template for reviewing your life across each of the life domains — I often use this template to get a broad snapshot of how I am travelling, to figure out where I might need to refocus my energy. This section takes you beyond that spring-clean we talked about to a lifestyle that supports your well-being and happiness.

Pacing yourself

On this journey, you may fly along merrily or pace yourself gently. Working to make changes in your life is not always an easy task, but it's not always hard either. Regardless of whether the changes you want to make are big or small, taking that first step (or even half-step) is what's important.

Often, small things can create dramatic changes. You might have heard of the butterfly effect. Edward Lorenz, the founder of chaos theory, said that the fluttering of a butterfly's wings might create tiny changes in the atmosphere, which could ultimately alter the path of, accelerate or even prevent a tornado. The butterfly's wings represent a small change in your life, which causes a chain of events creating big changes. Had the butterfly not flapped its wings, who knows what might have happened?

How you make your journey is your choice. Perhaps work on one life domain at a time, at your own pace. You could work steadily through them one by one, or cycle through them as suits your life. You may wish to consider one domain each month. It depends on what you are trying to achieve and how much of a sense of urgency you feel.

The sections on being your own best friend, dressing and grooming, promoting health and wellbeing, and designing your living space, are right near the beginning of this book. That's because if you feel good, you are more likely to be motivated to try new things. Increasing your physical energy and early enthusiasm will see you through the more difficult bits. Changes in these self-focused areas can quickly lift your confidence to tackle the bits that involve the outside world and other people, such as work and relationships. Start with something that matters to you, seems like it might be easy to try, and is something that you can see yourself succeeding at.

If there was one thing you could change in your life that would make the greatest impact on your overall happiness, what would it be? And what might be the first small step towards creating this change?

How will you best pace yourself to achieve your goals?

What order will work best for you?

Do you want to cover all the life domains in this book, or just some of them?

Answering the questions

Each topic in this book concludes with questions for you to consider. It would be easy to read the questions and not take the time to fully answer them. It would be easy to put them on your 'to do' list. Right now, take the first step and challenge the voice in your head that says, 'One day, I'll do all those things I've always wanted to do in my life' and make that 'one day' now. Have a go at answering the questions in rich detail, and not just thinking vaguely about them in your head.

There is a big difference between thinking, 'Hmm, that's a good question' and really trying to answer it. The process of puzzling together a response helps you build certainty in what you know and believe. Working through the questions will bring a clearer sense of what matters to you and a stronger conviction to make it a priority. Finding the answers helps you to create a clearer vision of your future and decide just how that picture will look. This is important!

You don't need to answer every question: just those that are right for you. If the questions don't seem to be the right ones at that time, ask yourself:

What do I need to consider most?

What is the right question for me, where the answer will bring about the changes I need?

Or simply ask yourself: What will bring about the greatest amount of happiness for me?

Pay close attention to the wording of the questions. Listen to what they are asking. If the question says, 'What would you like to see differently?', try to describe how things would be different in a positive sense. Avoid getting bogged down in endless lists of what you don't want. If you feel you need to go down this track then try to bring yourself to a point where your answer says, '… and what I *do* want instead is …'

How you answer the questions is up to you, depending on whether you are a words person or a visual person; whether you work better on your own or prefer working with others.

Would you prefer to answer the questions verbally or on paper?

If you are verbal, how could you record your answers?

If you choose to write your answers, would you prefer to keep

a journal, use an online blog or write yourself letters? Do you prefer writing by hand or typing?

Is there another way you'd like to keep track of your progress?

Be creative

Throughout this book you'll find 'creative challenges' where I ask you to make an artwork or to try some other creative activity, like writing a story, to help you envisage the life you want to make. You might not have drawn since you were at school, but that's okay — they can be simple pictures. You don't need to be artistic to have a go: think of stick figures, abstract shapes or symbols (like a clock to symbolise time). I've included these activities to help you draw on much more of your brain's amazing capacity than you would using only words and logic.

You only need simple art materials to create a drawing, painting or collage. For a drawing, you need no more than pencils. For a collage, you need a range of magazines, scissors and glue. If you prefer to get messy, you can use oil or chalk pastels, paint, charcoal or even clay. You could also use photography or any other media.

Making art can be a good way to fill in the details of your imagined picture of the future. It's the story of your picture that's important, the process of making it and what it means, not how good a piece of art it is. This is not about making art to frame and put on the walls (unless you want to do that).

I completed the exercises using a scrapbook, but you could use a plain paper journal. I drew a picture for each of the life domains in this book. In this way, I was visualising how I would like my future to be.

A word of encouragement

I am happy that you're willing to experiment with answering the questions in this book to bring greater happiness to your life. I hope you find the structure useful and that this will be a positive experience for you to plan and bring about a happier life. I also hope you find the journey itself rewarding and that you're surprised by what you are able to achieve. Perhaps you're already feeling more optimistic and hopeful?

This book was developed by reviewing research on happiness, listed in the references at the end. It was also influenced by my studies: four Masters degrees, in psychology, art therapy, public health and management. The questions in this book have come from my experience working as a psychologist with people who wanted to improve their lives. I found that they love the positive forward-looking style of the solution-focused approach.

You might also like to know that I got a lot out of writing this book. I've tried and tested the questions and creative activities in this book, and have chosen to share with you those that most helped me create happiness and meaning in my life.

While much of this book is about identifying goals and making deliberate choices to bring about a life based on meaning, it's important to remember it's the process, not the product, that is most important. Happiness is not so much a goal as a consequence of how we live from moment to moment. Happiness is not found so much in reaching your goal as in striving for it. It is more about your journey than your destination.

What are the signs your life is getting happier already?

PART 1

The Journey

| WHAT MAKES YOU **HAPPY?**

Take a peek at the
big picture

Happiness is a form of courage. Holbrook Jackson

Have you ever imagined your life from a bird's-eye view? Swoop back and take a peek at the big picture. Birds get to see things from a great perspective. I have always loved flying for this reason; when I am up in the clouds I can mentally float above my life, look down and think: Am I heading in the right direction? Am I doing what I really want to be doing? And most importantly, what makes me happy?

Don't wait until life becomes tougher than you can handle to realise that it's time to act in some way. Be brave and tackle the big questions — now!

What do you like about your life?

When are you happiest?

What gives you a sense of purpose?

What compliment would you most like to receive?

If you saw a shooting star what would you wish for?

Plan for a miracle

Some people see things the way they are and ask why?
I dream things that never were and ask why not?

George Bernard Shaw

Before you can do something, you need to be able to imagine it. One of the best ways to begin anything is to start with the end in mind. The Miracle Question is a tool that helps you construct a concrete vision of a preferred future so that you can begin to work towards it. Insoo Kim Berg developed the Miracle Question along with her colleagues, including Steve de Shazer, in the early 1980s.[1] Commonly used by solution-focused counsellors, it's a great way to visualise your preferred future.

The Miracle Question

Suppose you finish your day in the usual way, doing the things you usually do, and there comes a time when the day is done — or you're just too tired to do anymore. And you go to bed, and while you are sleeping and the house is quiet … a miracle happens. And the miracle is that all of the challenges you were facing before you went to sleep have been resolved, just like that! However, because you are sleeping you can't know that the miracle has happened. So …

When you wake up, you notice that you simply feel much happier. What is it that will tell you that a miracle has happened and that all your challenges have been resolved?

How will you discover that this miracle has happened to you?

How will your best friend discover that this miracle happened to you?

Has there been a time you can remember when things felt a bit like the miracle had happened?

Visualise a happier and **brighter future**

Imagination is more important than knowledge. Albert Einstein

It's never too late to make small changes in your life towards a happier and brighter future — life is too short to take for granted.

Part of moving forward is knowing where you are heading. The pictures we create in our mind of our future provide us with goals. And once we can see a happier and brighter future, we can make good choices about how to get there because we only need to consider one question: Is this choice moving me towards happiness?

Our goals don't need to be set in stone — you can always change your goals if, along the way, you find there's something more important you want to focus on.

Sometimes your goals may seem beyond your grasp; perhaps you worry that you're dreaming too big. What's surprising is that often, when we look back from our place on the journey, we find that the challenges we thought were insurmountable or the goals that seemed too far away were more easily achieved than we ever dreamed. Sometimes we surprise ourselves in what we are able to achieve.

Was there a time in the past when you would have been surprised about where you are now?

Suppose a similar change were possible in the future, what might be possible?

What will you be doing differently?

What might a cherished friend wish for you?

What are you looking forward to?

CREATIVE CHALLENGE

Here's the first of our creative challenges. I hope you find these challenges inspiring and motivating and that they help you to see your life from a different perspective. Remember, there's no right or wrong, good or bad.

Make an artwork (draw, paint, make a collage or whatever feels right for you) or write a 50-word story about all the things you want to keep in your present life. While thinking about what you want to change, think about what you like about yourself and your life right now, and what you might want more of.

- **What do you notice about how you feel while you are busy with this creative challenge?**

- **What do you notice about what already pleases you about yourself and your life?**

- **What can you build into your daily routines to support these good parts of your life?**

- **What activities can you practise to encourage these aspects of your life to become stronger?**

Get a better **life balance**

*As for the future, your task is not to foresee it,
but to enable it.* Antoine de Saint-Exupery

Sometimes keeping your life in balance feels like walking a tightrope — it's not easy when your life is overstuffed. As soon as we focus on balancing one area, we neglect another and things start to fall over. And while choosing to put more energy into one area of your life for a while may be okay, ultimately you will still find yourself asking: Have I got the balance right?

Think about all the different parts of your life, all the roles you play, and all the things you do. You might like to consider the life domains as they are divided up in this book. How much time do you spend on each life domain or activity in an average day?

Let's get a clear picture of where our time goes. Take a piece of paper and draw two circles — just like the ones opposite. These circles are your daily-life pie charts. The whole pie chart represents 24 hours.

How you spend your time is an expression of what is important in your life. In the first circle, draw slices of the pie to represent how much time you spend each day on particular aspects of your life, right now (your old life balance). Sleep is important to your overall wellbeing, so include it. If you are not sure how you spend your time or want to really get it right, consider keeping a diary for a day or two.

Now, think about how you would like the second circle (your new life balance) to look. What aspects of your life would you like to give more energy and attention (e.g. family, community, exercise, leisure) and where would you like to free up time and energy (e.g. work, TV viewing etc.)? You don't need to make large shifts — you might just want to put more emphasis on the small things that are important to you and that you enjoy. Draw the slices of the pie to show a new life balance that will help contribute to your wellbeing and happiness.

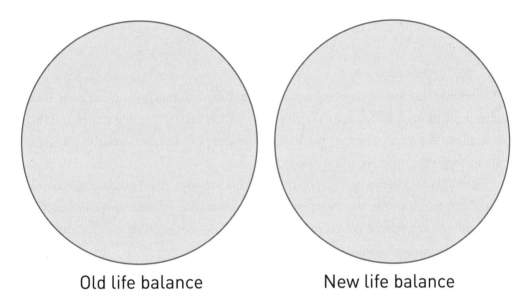

Old life balance   New life balance

How is your time currently divided between the activities of your day?

How can you free up time to create more of what you want in your life?

What do you want to increase your focus on?

How can you simplify your life?

Don't tough it out alone

Alone we can do so little; together we can do so much. Helen Keller

Sometimes, the easiest way to get something done is to tackle it on our own. It can be more difficult taking into account other people's ways of doing things and their preferences. But often, when we work with others, we can achieve something so much richer and greater than we could alone.

Ubuntu is an African philosophy that, at its heart, says, 'I am because you are and we are.' It reminds us that we create and maintain our sense of who we are through our relationships with others. We get our strength from our connection to those around us and to humankind as a whole.

Seek out people who will support you on your journey to make changes. One of the nicest things about partnering with others is that they can delight with you in your achievements. When others notice change, their feedback and encouragement help us consolidate our changing view of ourselves.

Also think about how you will maintain relationships with important people as you make changes. Making changes in your life can alter the way you relate to other people. While you are determined to make a change, what if the thing you want to change most is the thing they want to keep the same? Ideally, try to surround yourself with people who want you to be everything you can be, and who will joyfully welcome the person you are becoming.

Who encourages you to be at your best?

Who helps you to stand up to whatever problems you face?

When have others given you the confidence to do something you have otherwise felt unable to do?

What resources in the community could be useful to you?

How do you ask for help?

Use past experience
as a **future resource**

Research your own experiences, absorb what is useful,
reject what is useless, add what is specifically your own. Bruce Lee

We all experience challenges. When faced with any life situation or challenge, the most useful thing you can do is to stop and think about what has worked (or not) in the past. That way you can build on past experience by remembering how you overcame past challenges and find the skills you can take with you into the future. We learn valuable lessons from reflecting on what has worked in the past so we can do it again. Of course, when you discover that something doesn't work, trying something different next time is wiser!

Think about some of the challenges you have faced. How have you dealt with challenges so far?

What's different about you when things are going better?

What supports and resources have helped you to manage?

What will you do differently in the future?

How are you already doing those things?

Make a **clear plan**

True life is lived when tiny changes occur. Leo Tolstoy

For many, achieving a dream or goal can be elusive. Don't let this be the case with you. Pin down your dreams by developing a clear plan.

Goals don't have to be grand. Your goal might be to sort out your wardrobe, begin a new exercise program or learn a new skill.

First be clear about what you want to accomplish. Why is this important now? What will the benefits be if you do it? Who will benefit from this project? How will you and they know you've been successful?

You're much more likely to reach your goal if it's SMART:

Specific — What will you do exactly? In what order will you do it?

Measurable — How will you measure your success? How will you know you have achieved your goal?

Achievable — How will you achieve the goal? Who will work with you? What resources do you need to meet your goal?

Realistic — What tells you this goal is do-able? What could go wrong? How will you cope if that happens?

Time-limited — When do you want to have achieved the goal by?

When you're clear about what you want to achieve, decide on your course of action. Plan the sequence in which things will be done: if you're working with others, decide who will do what; work out how long each step will take; work out what resources you need (new running shoes? art supplies? packing boxes?); and calculate how much will it cost. Include tactics and logistics in your planning. Think about risks to meeting your goals (what could stand in your way?) and how you might manage these risks.

Next, put the plan into action. As you work towards your goal, you'll need to keep an eye on your progress. Along the way, you might hit hurdles or roadblocks you didn't anticipate. Your challenge then is to work out what you can do to get the plan back on track. Change your plan if you need to — it's not set in concrete. If you're working with a group, keep talking to each other and offer support and encouragement.

When you've achieved your goal, celebrate! Take some time to enjoy your accomplishment. And by reflecting on your achievements, you can learn from any mistakes and know what works best for next time. What did you learn that was unexpected?

Think about a project that went well from start to finish. What did you and others do to make it a success?

How did you respond to the challenges that came along?

What do you think is worth taking forward to guide you in future projects?

Do something you've been putting off

Take the first step in faith. You don't have to see the whole staircase, just take the first step. Martin Luther King Jr

Is procrastination stopping you from achieving your dreams? Procrastination is very common. Instead of doing what we really want to do, we spend time doing something else. But it is never too late to start out on your journey.

Today, more than ever, there are countless distractions to grab our attention and give us instant gratification. In our society, it's very easy to find things to watch, listen to or do, any time of the day or night. But perhaps something else is getting in the way: a fear that things will not go well, that it will be too hard, that we might not see it through. Stress builds up when we put things off.

Challenge your excuses and justifications. Focus on what excites you about the task and why it is important to you. Visualise what you want to achieve and how good it is to tick things off your to-do list. And if you find one of the reasons you've been putting off a task is that it's not really important, don't feel guilty about scrapping it from your list.

Break the task down into manageable parts and decide how long you will spend on each. Remove potential distractions and get started. Focus. Take the first step (or half-step) and then the next. Keep focused on the piece you are working on right now, not the entire task.

Ultimately nothing gets done if you don't start. So if there's something to do, do it. If not, relax and have fun!

What are the excuses that get in the way of what you want to achieve?

How can you overcome the things that get in the way of achieving your goals?

How do you challenge yourself to step outside your comfort zone?

What is the one thing you would like to achieve this year?

Develop five daily
happiness habits

*We are what we repeatedly do. Excellence, then,
is not an act, but a habit.* Aristotle

How many happiness-making activities do you do on a daily basis? There are many simple and enjoyable activities we can build into daily life that bring fulfilment, enjoyment and energy.

Plan five daily habits you would like to establish as part of your routine. You might include virtuous things (like doing 30 minutes of exercise, or drinking green tea), nurturing activities (like doing something kind for someone), relaxing activities (like reading a book), or activities that are just plain fun (like a long chat on the telephone or eating with your fingers). Choose things that will build your health, wellbeing and happiness.

The challenge many people face is embedding these happiness-making activities in their daily routine. Use the checklist below to monitor your progress by placing a tick in the box when you have practised your delicious daily habit. Choose a day when you think you can get off to a good start (some people find Monday too stressful to start new habits) and record the days of the week in the top row. See if you can keep it up for a whole week; chances are if you do, some delicious daily habits will already be built into your routine.

What activities, large or small, would enhance your everyday happiness?

What are five delicious daily habits you would like to have as part of your routine?

My 5 Delicious Daily Habits	Mon	Tues	Wed	Thur	Fri	Sat	Sun

Develop healthy and **happiness-making** routines

Great things are done by a series of small things brought together. Vincent Van Gogh

Have you ever thought to yourself: If I could just do less of this and more of that, I'd be a whole lot happier? Perhaps there is something you would like to leave behind, or that you give yourself a hard time for doing? One of the best ways to reduce an unwanted activity is to regularly do things you'd prefer to be doing instead.

Routines can be a good way to get into the habit of doing something regularly, especially if you are taking on something new. Routines also remove decision-making opportunities: in each moment of indecision, there is the risk you will not choose the better option. So, by reducing the number of times a day we have to make a choice, we can increase the likelihood of doing things that we know will make us healthier and happier.

I like to use a calendar like the one on the following page to plan those things I want to spend more time doing regularly. By scheduling time for those things I want to do — making an appointment with myself — I'm more likely to do them. An electronic diary and reminder system works well for some people. Think about ways you can be creative with your time: travelling to work, or your lunch break, might be the ideal time to learn a new skill or exercise.

If you find set routines a bit boring, begin to think of them as patterns that free up energy and time. Anything that is part of your routine is less of a drain on your energy and can usually be done more quickly than if it were a one-off event. If you are seriously boring-phobic, try developing a new plan at the beginning of each week. Or you could set targets for the week like 'walking 30 minutes each day' and mark down when you walk to keep track of how you are meeting your goals. Challenge your need for flexibility, if it gets in the way of achieving your goals.

What would a realistic yet balanced, healthy and happy lifestyle look like as a weekly routine?

If you felt more organised and in control of your life, what would your daily routine look like?

What can you do in the next week that will bring about extra happiness?

Health and Happiness-Making Routine

	Mon	Tues	Wed	Thur	Fri	Sat	Sun
Early Morning							
Late Morning							
Midday							
Early Afternoon							
Late Afternoon							
Evening							
Night							

Write a list

If you want to be fast, go slow. Lao Tzu

Do you ever feel stressed thinking about all the things you need to do? Life seems to get busier and busier and we seem to have less and less time. Lists offer us a great way to free up time and energy. They help you keep track of priorities and free your brain from having to remember so many things. You might also like to think of a to-do list as an 'accomplishment list' — have a celebratory moment as you tick things off your list.

Write down everything you want to achieve — big or small — and prioritise each one as high, medium or low. High priority means it needs to be done within the next day. Decide for yourself the right timeframes for medium – and low-priority items. Balance importance with urgency — those things that are the most urgent are not necessarily the most important. Make time for things that are important but not urgent.

If a goal seems too overwhelming or complex, try thinking about the first step or half-step and about what supports or resources might help. Start with the thing that is most do-able and likely to bring beneficial change.

Challenge procrastination if putting things off just makes you more frustrated. Allocate time for achieving tasks on your list. Be as efficient and effective as possible, and then take time off. Make sure you have list-free time as well.

How can you do more of what will bring you greater happiness?

How can you increase the time you spend on important things even if there is no urgency to complete them?

How can you decrease the time you spend on unimportant things?

What is one small thing you can do that will help you change the balance of how you spend your time?

✓	Task	Importance	Due Date

Do less

Nature does not hurry, yet everything is accomplished. Lao Tzu

Do more of what makes you happy by doing less. Researchers have found that people who always feel rushed are less likely to be happy than people who almost never feel rushed.[2]

One way of doing less is to get better at saying 'no'. Many people find it a challenge to say 'no' to others. Try using these three steps: first, acknowledge the request; second, explain your reason for declining the request (if you need to give a reason); and third, say 'no' — and mean it!

Sometimes people get in the habit of letting others make decisions for them. Instead, take responsibility for your own decisions. You do not need to apologise for saying 'no'.

A great way to say 'no' is to use the slightly old-fashioned, 'Thank you, but I prefer not to.' This allows everyone to withdraw while saving face.

You can do less in many ways — it's not just about saying no to requests. Choose to walk instead of driving in rush-hour traffic. Talk less and listen more. Work smarter, not harder. Wherever you can, cut down on meetings and have more time for your most important tasks. Buy less, be in less debt, have less clutter and more space. Plan less. Worry less. Do less.

The choice is yours. By slowing down you will have more time to appreciate the beauty around you. Live a calmer and more peaceful life by simply doing less.

How can you do less?

What steps do you need to take to make your life flow more effortlessly and easily?

Get a clearer perspective

Life is really simple, but we insist on making it complicated. Confucius

Change can seem complicated. We visualise the benefits of making changes in our life, but even as we dream, we are aware of the downsides of change. Staying where we are can be attractive because it's easy — nothing is required of us and we can just keep doing what we are doing. Change looks scary and a lot like hard work.

But there are also downsides to keeping things the same. It may not be supporting us on our journey to happiness. Weighing up the benefits and risks of change can be useful if you are ambivalent or finding it hard to commit to change. Counsellors working with people who want to make all sorts of changes in their lives commonly use the questions in the exercise below to help clarify things.[3]

The purpose of this exercise is to have an honest and open look at the ways your current behaviour might meet your needs and hold you back at the same time. It acknowledges that change is rarely straightforward, and that change requires us to lose something that we once found useful. Sometimes, acknowledging that change is not simple in fact makes change easier.

How can you encourage yourself to take steps to increase happiness in your life?

Stay the Same	Try Something New
POSITIVE What are the positive things about staying the same?	What are the positive things about changing?
NEGATIVE What are the negative things about staying the same?	What are the negative things about changing?

Know what motivates you

If I have the belief that I can do it, I shall surely acquire the capacity to do it even if I may not have it at the beginning. Mahatma Gandhi

When you try something new, what motivates you to keep going? We can draw motivation from many sources and in a number of ways. And the more sources of motivation you draw on, the better.

Some people are more motivated to participate in activities where they can socialise and have fun with others, whereas some prefer to try new things on their own. Does receiving positive comments from others help keep you motivated? Are you more motivated if other people are relying on you? If you wanted to increase your physical activity, for example, would you be more committed to a team sport or would you prefer a solitary walk or jog?

When it comes to change, different approaches keep different people engaged too. Some people need clear instructions on how to achieve change, whereas others prefer to dive in and work things out as they go. Do you like to gather lots of information and plan your approach before making any changes to your lifestyle? Would developing new skills help you to succeed? If so, enrolling in a course, enlisting the support of a coach, or joining a class may be the key to sustained change.

Some people thrive on routine as a way of sustaining a new activity, such as exercise, while others loathe it. Do you prefer to work at your own pace to achieve your goals? Or do you get bored and need a range of activities and strategies to keep you motivated? Knowing what works for you will help you find the right sources of motivation.

What motivates you?

What builds your determination to achieve your goals?

What helps you persist until you achieve what you set out to do?

Flex your wings

What the caterpillar calls the end of the world, the master calls a butterfly. Richard Bach

Struggle is part of the transformation process. Helpful struggle has a purpose — think about a butterfly struggling to leave its cocoon. The butterfly flexes its wings against the cocoon's constraints, pushing and working its wings, getting them ready for flight. A man, who feels sorry for the struggling butterfly, opens the cocoon to let it out more easily. But the butterfly's wings did not stretch and dry and so now it cannot fly, and instead remains on the ground, vulnerable.

Visualising your preferred future can help you to stay positive and keep your motivation alive, but it's not enough by itself. Change is about actively working through and engaging with challenges to build a happier and brighter future.

Reaching a state of wellbeing and happiness doesn't mean that your life will be trouble-free. The goal is to have the confidence you need to find a way to overcome adversity, and to find the support you need to do this. We need challenges so we can practise coping in tough situations. They make us stronger and better equipped to deal with other hurdles in the future. Every challenge brings opportunities, so learn to look for them.

What have past challenges taught you about what is important?

How do these past experiences make the future seem more possible?

Which of your strengths do you call on to get you through difficult times?

How will these skills and qualities show themselves in the future?

What might you come to appreciate about the challenges in your life?

PART 2

Life Domains

WHAT MAKES YOU **HAPPY?**

DOMAIN 1:
Being your own best friend

This above all; to thine own self be true. William Shakespeare

How many people treat themselves with as much care and kindness as they treat their best friend? The relationship you have with yourself — how you think about yourself and what you say to yourself — is essential to your self-esteem.

Make time, aside from the business of the day, to care for yourself. Meditate or practise relaxation to reduce stress. You might have your own relaxation space at home, or you could sit in a park, or use your 'thinking time' on public transport, while fishing, surfing or going for a walk.

Take time to appreciate what is going well in your life and look with hope towards a brighter future. Use this reflection time to get to know yourself better. Spend time thinking about your values and the things that bring meaning to your life, as well as what you are grateful for. Think about and appreciate your strengths and identify ways you can use them to their full potential.

You can use this time to plan how you will manage your priorities, determining those things that you need to invest energy in and those that are not worth worrying too much about. It might also be a time when you reflect on the questions in this book and plan how to create extra happiness in your life.

Caring for yourself is not selfish. In fact, it's only when we refill our own cups that we can give to others. You've heard people say that you have to love yourself before you can truly love others. Well, this is what they are talking about. It's the same reason we're told on planes to fit our own oxygen mask before helping others: we're no use to anyone if we're not breathing ourselves! When we're okay, we can connect fully with others. And caring for other people can help us feel even better about ourselves.

If you had a personal motto or song what would it be?

When are you at your best?

What are you proud of?

What do your friends like about you?

What helps you to feel strong?

CREATIVE CHALLENGE

Can you remember a time recently when you were feeling content, strong, safe and relaxed? Try to recall the details about the place and how you were feeling in your body.

Make an artwork that represents you and how you feel when you are calm and relaxed. You might like to make a collage so you can use texture as well as colour and shape to express yourself.

If you're musical, you might like to compose a piece of music that expresses your calm and relaxed way of being. You could try humming this to yourself when you next need to draw on your calm and relaxed self.

Make **today** special

Attitude is a little thing that makes a big difference. Winston Churchill

Look for ways to make each day special. Children are great at reminding us that playfulness and humour make life fun. We should all be instructed to 'go outside and play' more often. Be a kid, sing loudly, run, pull faces and do silly walks.

Humour is a great way to connect with others and to see things with a different perspective. Laughter releases endorphins and is infectious — it radiates energy to others. Surround yourself with people and things that make you laugh: see films, read books, go to a comedy show … do anything that is likely to make you smile.

Plan to have fun despite your circumstances and don't wait for fun to happen to you. Find that thing that makes you laugh. When you can make fun out of visiting the accountant, or waiting in traffic, you know that you can make fun anywhere.

We all face choices about how we view our lives, the people around us, and our future. Adopting a positive approach to life and our future involves prioritising happiness in our life, making plans to be happy, and doing things that promote wellbeing and happiness as often as possible.

Imagine at the end of the day you said, 'I had a really enjoyable day, even though it was just an ordinary day'. What would you have done?

When does it help to not take life too seriously?

What helps you to get yourself out of a bad mood?

What helps you to see the funny side of life?

How do you bring play and enjoyment into your daily life?

What makes you laugh?

Name **one thing** you are grateful for each day

We must find time to stop and thank the people who make a difference in our lives. Dan Zandra

Instead of focusing on everything you don't like about your life and that you want to change, consider all the things you do like about your life. Taking the time to really appreciate what is going well and what feels good about you and your life can help you strengthen these aspects further.

People who perceive a large gap between what they have and what they want (whether it's money, a job, friends, health) are unhappier than those who perceive the gap is smaller.[4] Feeling gratitude and appreciation for the qualities, relationships and things we do have — especially the simple pleasures — can bring great happiness.

In our house, we reflect on our day by sharing a good thing that happened over dinner. Our kids often find this easy, whereas the grown-ups can struggle at times. One evening, my partner rattled off four bad things that had happened to him that day. The youngest, six years old at the time, quickly said, 'Dad, now you're going to have to have five good things to balance out the bad things.' My partner thought of one good thing and then got stuck. The rest of the family helped him find more good things.

At the end of each day, it can be a lovely routine to name something that has given you happiness. Be grateful for what is already going well and the things you are looking forward to. As some people say, 'Happiness is wanting what we have, rather than having what we want.'

What are you thankful for?

What are everyday things that you enjoy doing?

What small things make your days happier?

What and who do you want to acknowledge for creating happiness in your life?

What is currently going well? What difference has this made?

How have you contributed towards those things you appreciate? And what does that tell you about yourself?

> ## INSPIRING IDEA
>
> I was delighted to learn some friends have created a happy-thoughts jar. Everyone gets involved by contributing happy thoughts — things they are grateful for or enjoy doing together. The youngest draws pictures instead of writing her ideas. If anyone in the family is grumpy or feeling down, they get out the happy-thoughts jar. What a happy thought!

Build **confidence**
one step at a time

Optimism is the faith that leads to achievement.
Nothing can be done without hope and confidence. Helen Keller

Often we are most limited by our own lack of faith. If we don't believe in ourselves, we are not confident in what we can offer others — and our relationships suffer.

Having confidence means being hopeful for a positive outcome and visualising success. Confidence is key to achieving our happiness goals. For many, feeling confident is also an aspect of being happy.

Confidence helps us to engage in relationships, take risks and try new things. And, when we feel confident, we start to realise that we can often achieve much more than we think we can.

Since confidence is so important to achieving our goals, let's take a closer look at our confidence levels. The following exercise uses scaling. Scaling is a tool you can use to make abstract and vague ideas more concrete. It brings ideas alive and turns them into something you can work with and change. Scaling your confidence helps you to look at what small changes would bring about an increase in confidence.[5]

Draw a line across a page, and write the numbers 1 to 10 beneath the line. Place a cross on the line at the number you think represents how confident you are that you're on the right track to meet your happiness goals. On the scale, 1 means you're not confident at all and 10 means you thoroughly believe you are on the right track. Repeat the exercise every now and then as you begin to make changes and see how your success affects your confidence.

What tells you that you are at this level?

What is different about being at this level compared to being at a lower level?

How have you been able to maintain this level of confidence?

What would it take for you to move one point higher on the scale?

Suppose you move one point higher on the scale, how will you know? What will you be doing differently?

Be kind to yourself

Be wise. Treat yourself, your mind, sympathetically, with loving kindness. If you are gentle with yourself, you will become gentle with others. Lama Thubten Yeshe

How we talk to ourselves in our head directly influences our happiness. Over the course of our life, we can fill our heads with negative self-statements like, 'I never do anything right' or 'I'm too fat for people to like me.' These statements repeat automatically in our heads whenever we experience something that makes us doubt ourselves or our abilities. These statements may have stuck with us from something someone once said, or we may have picked them up from the media. Or maybe they are just something we have come to believe about ourselves based on a range of experiences.

People with low self-esteem often say negative things to themselves. Self-esteem is based on the picture we have of ourselves (our self-concept) and our beliefs about what we should be like (our ideal self).[6] A person with low self-esteem has only a few of the characteristics they believe they should have, while a person with high self-esteem believes they have most of the characteristics they regard as ideal. So while we have goals about becoming a better person, our self-concept and picture of our ideal self may not fully overlap, and this is fine.

Ways to improve self-esteem include being kind to yourself, having confidence in your potential, and drawing on your strengths. Choose to avoid negative people and actively ignore pessimists, including your own internal critic — who is often the harshest. Try not to compare yourself with others and accept that not everyone will always like the things you like.

Listen to the automatic thoughts that run through your head, and if you catch yourself saying something negative, try to add 'until now' at the end: 'I never do anything right, until now.' 'I'm too fat for people to like me, until now.'

Examine the evidence for your self-statements. Ask yourself, 'Is this really true?' and if so, 'Is it true all of the time?' How would a good friend answer these questions? Develop some positive statements that you can use to replace the negative ones each time you catch that voice starting its criticisms.

Surround yourself with people who view you positively. Free your mind of negative self-talk and give yourself permission to feel good about *you*.

> **What ideas or experiences influence the way you see yourself? Are they helpful or unhelpful or a bit of both?**
>
> **If you were to see yourself through the eyes of significant people in your life, what do you think they most appreciate about you?**
>
> **When do you feel special?**
>
> **How do you encourage yourself?**
>
> **What enriches you?**
>
> **What is something positive you could do for yourself in the next week?**

Take some 'me' time

Wherever you go, go with all your heart. Confucius

Spending time alone, just being with yourself, is loathed by some and cherished by others. If you're in the first group, try to think about why you find 'me' time uncomfortable. There's great value in taking a little time out from others and from hectic activity. Time alone may become part of a reflective process. Time alone may also be used for a personal project or a favourite pastime.

Sitting on a porch of an evening may be a time for listening to yourself and remembering what is important in your life. Time for self-reflection can allow us to learn from our own experience. It can also help us to assess our potential and our future possibilities. What you focus on grows; acknowledging positive qualities, achievements and skills fertilises their growth. Only when we give time to ourselves are we then available to give to others.

One way to develop your skill of self-reflection is to keep a journal. Sei Shōnagon's *The Pillow Book*, written around 1000 AD, is a collection of personal thoughts and lists centred around anecdotes and character sketches of the early Japanese court and its religious ceremonies. Why not create your own 'pillow book' and write lists of whatever takes your fancy: complimentary things; elegant things or 'things that make the heart beat faster'; inspiring things, things that bring about a state of wonderment; disagreeable things, things that bring inconvenience; or things that bring a simple comfort.

There are so many ways of looking at the world, taking a different angle for a moment can help put things into perspective.

You can also try keeping a journal to reflect on daily events. You might use it to record the positive or happy things that happened to you over the day or to list the things you are feeling particularly grateful for. You can use it to capture your hopes and dreams. One of my friends keeps a diary in which she documents what her children mean to her and what they have contributed to her life.

A journal can also act as a 'worry box', a place where you can list your concerns so you can put them aside. Some people like to explore writing poetry or short stories. Others may use a journal to express their feelings or puzzle through difficulties.

Your journal should be as individual as you are. You can keep a scrapbook, make a video diary, write a blog, or keep a written or photographic journal. However you choose to do it, make it uniquely yours.

> **How much time do you set aside to be with yourself? What do you usually do?**
>
> **How could you use time alone to bring extra happiness to your life?**
>
> **What might you learn about yourself, your values, and what's important to you in this time?**
>
> **What is the best way for you to reflect on your own experiences and make positive changes in your life?**

Appreciate
your strengths

We tend to forget that happiness doesn't come as a result of getting something we don't have, but rather of recognising and appreciating what we do have. Friedrich Koenig

Strengths help people manage the things that go wrong — and strengths can be cultivated. While we can always try to reduce our weaknesses, we can also work on using and building our strengths, our positive qualities and attributes. It's probably best to aim for both, but making the best use of our strengths is likely to be easier and more enjoyable. So, in the spirit of doing enjoyable things, let's take some time to think about our positive qualities.

Read through the list of strengths overleaf. Think carefully about what the words mean to you, then choose your top five strengths. It can be difficult to choose, but try to whittle down the list until you have just five strengths that you believe are your most positive attributes. Remember, no person would tick everything on this list, nor should you give yourself a hard time for not having selected some of the strengths listed.

Knowing what you are good at is important in appreciating and using your strengths. Then, develop your skills, talents and abilities so you can use them more in your life. This is your gift to yourself and the world.

Accepting
Adventurous
Appreciative
Assertive
Authentic
Calm
Careful
Committed
Confident
Content
Cooperative
Courageous
Creative
Curious
Empathic
Energetic
Enthusiastic

Fair
Forgiving
Generous
Gracious
Thankful
Honest
Hopeful
Humorous
Independent
Insightful
Inspiring
Intimate
Joyful
Kind
Loving
Loyal
Mature

Open-minded
Optimistic
Passionate
Patient
Peaceful
Perseverant
Playful
Purposeful
Reflective
Resilient
Self-controlled
Supportive
Tolerant
Trusting
Visionary
Wise

What are your top qualities, skills and attributes?

What have others noticed you are good at? How do you project your qualities?

How do these strengths help you in your daily life? When are they most useful?

What strengths do you appreciate in your friends, family and workmates?

How do you let your friends, family and workmates know that you notice their strengths and appreciate these qualities in them?

Communicate clearly and **confidently**

Happiness depends upon ourselves. Aristotle

How good are you at keeping calm when things heat up? It can be difficult to hold our tongue when we're upset or offended, but for the sake of our happiness, it's important. Next time you are offended by something or someone, stop and think.

Aim to respond rather than to react. Give yourself time before responding because often, in the heat of the moment, we say things we live to regret. If you are angry, it's most likely that people will see only your anger and not hear what is important to you. Think through the possibilities and different ways of seeing a situation. It might be helpful to take some time out to think about what has happened, in order to reflect and take some deep breaths. This will help you frame a positive response rather than a hasty reaction.

When you've thought about what you want to achieve by responding, and are ready to confront the issue, speak calmly and clearly and check your body language and tone of voice. Practise assertiveness.

Assertiveness means communicating your needs, wants, feelings, beliefs and opinions to other people in a clear and direct manner, while still respecting other perspectives. A good way to understand assertiveness is to differentiate it from being passive or aggressive.

A passive response is to avoid conflict and to not speak up when you're offended, angered or your needs aren't being considered. The trouble with passivity is that others have no idea about your views, and therefore won't value your needs. You end up feeling helpless. If you find yourself saying, 'It doesn't matter to me' or using unconfident body language, assess whether you really do not mind or if you are just responding passively.

At the other extreme are people who always push for their needs to be met without compromise. This includes people who bully or push others around, possibly even using threats or yelling, and who use aggressive body language like waving a fist or banging tables.

The middle ground — being assertive — involves using direct and clear communication, speaking clearly and with confidence, while respecting others. Using statements like, 'What I would like is ... ', having confident body language, and listening to other people's points of view demonstrates assertiveness.

Being assertive means that you can manage your anger better, have your needs heard (and make it more likely they will be met), minimise conflict, and have better relationships.

How can you manage challenging situations in a more positive way?

What helps you to communicate more clearly and confidently?

Stress less

Within you there is a stillness and a sanctuary to which you can retreat at any time and be yourself. Hermann Hesse

Believe it or not, stress can be good for us: it helps us to try new things and step outside our comfort zone. Big events such as getting married or having a party can be stressful, but the stress is not enough to stop us going through with them. How you experience stress depends on how demanding you perceive a situation to be and whether you have the resources to deal with those demands.

Whatever the cause of your stress, it does have physical and mental effects, so the best way to reduce or counteract these effects is to relax. Deliberate relaxation can help you to wind down when things are a bit hectic, and promote sleep. Going to sleep in a state of calmness rather than tension allows you to awake refreshed and ready to face the world anew.

One of my favourite exercises to help me relax is to focus on a favourite place. Lie on your back on a comfortable surface, close your eyes, and take a few slow, slightly deeper breaths. Imagine yourself in a beautiful place: one where you feel safe, relaxed and calm. Notice the surroundings. What kind of weather is it? What can you feel around you? What can you see? Are there any sounds? Concentrate on the images for a few minutes. If you imagine relaxing at the beach, for instance, think about the warmth of the sun, the sound of tumbling waves, the feel of the grains of sand and the smell of salt water. How does your body feel in this place?

To enhance your mood and reduce your stress you could also try drinking chamomile or other herbal teas; taking a luxurious footbath with rosemary and cinnamon oil; trying a relaxation massage; or yoga classes. If these methods work, keep using them. If they don't leave you feeling calmer and more in control, ask other people what they do to stress less and try any idea that appeals to you. Experiment until you find something that works for you.

Imagine a place where you feel relaxed, calm and strong. What does it look like?

What do you do to relax? What rejuvenates you?

What helps you to feel calm, clear and spacious within yourself?

How do you find inner calm in the face of outer chaos?

What will be different if there is less stress in your life?

Be. Here. Now

Smile, breathe and go slowly. Thich Nhat Hanh

Have you ever met someone who has struck you as being completely in tune with their surroundings? Often, they're described as being present or 'in the moment'. Being present — in the here and now — can have a dramatic effect on your happiness and contentment. It's called mindfulness, and meditation is one of the best ways to practise it.

Mindfulness is about being in the moment and becoming fully aware of what surrounds us and what goes on for us in our decision-making and actions. There's a simple exercise that can help you start exploring mindfulness. This activity will take about three minutes. I'm going to suggest you use a sultana, but you can use any other piece of fruit you like. First, hold the sultana. Feel its texture and look at the colour. Smell the sultana. Try not to think about it too much, just focus on being present and fully aware of the sultana. Next, put the sultana in your mouth, roll your tongue around the sultana, feeling the texture. Close your eyes and experience the taste of the sultana as you bite into it, focusing only on the sultana, remaining mindfully present.

How did you find the experience? Was it difficult for you to remain in the moment?

Now try this next meditation exercise. Close your eyes and pay close attention to your breathing. Focus on the sensation of your breath as it flows through your nostrils, into your lungs and then out again. Continue this for five or ten minutes, staying focused only on your breath. Whenever your mind wanders, bring your attention gently back to your breath. Thoughts will come; notice them, but don't latch onto them.

Let them float away and return your attention to your breath. By practising meditation many people find they develop a clearer state of mind and better awareness of the world.

You might like to join a meditation group or class to help you make the most of your practice. Alternatively, there are CDs and podcasts you can use to guide your practice at home.

After practising meditation for a while, you might notice that it becomes easier to slow down your mind and that the chatter in your head (some practitioners call it 'monkey mind') quietens more quickly.

Try being mindfully present during boring activities, such as when you are cleaning your home, practising being fully aware and present in each moment. Explore the stillness, simplicity and contentment of being in the moment.

What helps you to stay focused on the present?

What would support you to make meditation part of your daily routine?

How might being more aware and present make a difference in your life?

Practise compassion

If you want others to be happy, practise compassion.
If you want to be happy, practise compassion. Dalai Lama

We all need to feel loved and to know we belong. For many of us, though, there are times we doubt that people care and we wonder where we fit in. Our lives are so busy we find others (and ourselves) slipping down the priority list. We become focused on keeping up and getting ahead and we forget that, without love and a place where we can be ourselves, our lives lose meaning.

The Dalai Lama says that because we have become so focused on material wealth, we are neglecting to foster the attributes of kindness, compassion, cooperation and caring.[7] He says that for our own and others' happiness, we need to care about each other's wellbeing.

Some people would say the single best thing you can do to be happy is to practise compassion. Compassion means feeling deep sympathy and real sorrow for those who are suffering. Love and compassion are strongly associated with our happiness. Compassion gives us energy, determination and kindness, which all lead to forgiveness, inner strength and the confidence to overcome fear and adversity.

The good news is that we can increase our compassion for others. A common way to do this is through a meditation exercise that involves spreading compassion or 'loving kindness'.

To start, find a comfortable place to sit or lie. Once you are settled, focus on sending loving kindness to yourself; wish that you are well and happy. Stay with these thoughts for a few moments. Now, call to mind a friend, perhaps a very close friend. Imagine them sitting next to you and that you are wishing for them to be well and happy. When you are ready, think about someone you know only a little — perhaps a shopkeeper or someone you only just met. Wish that they, too, are well and happy. Now, bring to mind a person you have difficulty with. Many would say that this is the tricky bit. Consider that they, too, are a person who wants to be well and happy. Consider that they may be doing their best at this time, with the resources available to them, to be happy. Send them the wish to do well in their journey to happiness. Finally, broaden your well-wishing to include the whole planet: 'All people and animals in the world, may they be well and happy.'

How do you feel after this meditation?

After practising this meditation, how has the way you relate to others changed?

How do you show kindness and compassion?

INSPIRING IDEA

Each morning, when you wake up, say to yourself, 'May all beings be well and happy.'

Use your **moral compass**

*Happiness is when what you think, what you say,
and what you do are in harmony.* Mahatma Gandhi

Your values give you a framework for your thinking about the world and help you to decide what is important. They provide a moral compass and, in large part, determine your actions. Knowing your values makes it easier to make decisions. Having a clear sense of what matters enables us to know what to do and to have the resolve to do it. Values give us both conviction and commitment.

Often, there is a tension between our lifestyle and our values. Society's focus on a lifestyle characterised by owning the latest technological innovation, moving up in the world and achieving financial success doesn't sit well with our sense of what really matters. We know that being able to spend more time with family and friends, and having less stress and pressure in life, are more important to our happiness than having money to buy things.[8] But the tension itself can cause unhappiness.

Regularly taking the time to check your moral compass can help keep you on the path to happiness. When you feel the pressure to conform to external pressures or expectations about what is important, take the time to reflect how well these external pressures align with your internal values. Thinking carefully about your values and acting on them can help bring about a stronger sense of wellbeing and happiness.

Be determined to live by your values.

Below is a list of values. Not all of them will be important to you, and some of them you may even perceive as undesirable! Remember, everyone has different values. From the list, choose ten values that resonate strongly for you. Now comes the hard part: gradually refine the list until you have the five values that are most important to you.

Achievement	Fame	Mindfulness
Authenticity	Fortune	Peace
Autonomy	Friendship	Personal choice
Beauty	Generosity	Pride
Being admired	Greed	Prudence
Belonging	Having nice things	Public interest
Clear-headedness	Having power	Putting others first
Collaboration	High quality	Putting yourself first
Compassion	Honesty	Quality relationships
Competence	Hope	Reliability
Competition	Humility	Respect
Connecting with others	Humour	Restraint
Cooperation	Individuality	Social connectedness
Creativity	Indulgence	Social justice
Efficiency	Interdependency	Status
Equality	Intimacy	Sustainable living
Excellence	Kindness	Trustworthiness
Faith	Mateship	Truthfulness

What are you deeply passionate about?

What values does your family hold that you want to pass onto your children and significant others?

Believe in something bigger than yourself

The more you lose yourself in something bigger than yourself, the more energy you will have. Norman Vincent Peale

Many people believe in a higher power. Some people call their relationship with this higher power or being, faith, some call it religion, while others call it spirituality. Whatever people call this aspect of their lives, it is closely related to their values.

We've already explored how our values provide us with guidance about how to be in the world and how to treat others. Many people find their spirituality plays a guiding role in determining their actions.

A 2012 Gallup poll of more than 150 countries found that half of the world's population had visited a place of worship in the week prior to the survey[9] and studies have found that people who are spiritual or religious are happier and more satisfied with their lives.[4] Researchers exploring happiness have also found that people who are religious tend to have high on their priority list their family, helping others and voluntary work — and these things all increase our happiness.[10]

Spirituality has both personal and social aspects. People who practise their faith or spirituality tend to have a greater sense of meaning in their life and feel more respected. The spiritual or religious community can also offer a source of support and a sense of belonging, although sadly some religious organisations have not always welcomed all groups of people equally.

A belief in something more important than one's self also helps us to be more resilient during tough times. Those who embrace spirituality have less depression and greater wellbeing, especially in times of loss, such as the death of a loved one. Having a belief in something bigger than yourself can help you feel purposeful in your life.

What does spirituality mean to you? How do you cultivate spirituality in your life?

If spirituality is not part of your life, what do you draw comfort from? What helps you to maintain a sense of hope and optimism? What helps you to keep going through troubled times?

What has helped you form your values?

What helps create a sense of wonder?

My commitment to being my own best friend

What I like about how I currently spend my time alone is:

My goals for how I can be a better friend to myself are:

What has worked for me in the past is to:

Other sources of support and encouragement I can use are:

I can boost my confidence by:

My next step is to:

DOMAIN 2:
Dressing and grooming

And the day came when the risk to remain tight in the bud was more painful than the risk it took to blossom. Anaïs Nin

For both men and women, dressing and grooming is one of the life domains that can help give you a kick-start to feeling better about yourself. While there may be a temptation to see things such as fashion and hairstyles as superficial or only skin deep, it's a reality that self-confidence is linked with how we present ourselves to the world. And researchers have found that people rate their wellbeing higher when they feel well presented.[4]

Feeling confident about how you look can significantly enhance your happiness. It's one of those lovely reciprocal kinds of relationships where improvements in one area lead to enhancements in the other. But by the same token, neglecting one can undermine the other.

How we project ourselves to the world influences how we are in the world. Our appearance is important, not because we need to conform to someone else's idea of how people *should look*, but because our appearance projects our energy to the world. And when we want to let others know that we are making changes, a new haircut or colour or a new pair of glasses is a very noticeable statement of change.

We all have our individual personality — we are all different. Our appearance should be an expression of the self we most want to be. We don't need to wear the latest fashion, or spend huge amounts of money on someone else's idea of what looks good. We also don't need to spend hours in front of the mirror. It's about honouring our inner beauty by taking the time to consider and plan how we project ourselves to the people around us.

How could you improve the way you dress?

Although you may not ask them directly, what would your friends, partner, family or workmates say about your clothes?

Imagine you are leaving your house and feeling fabulous about how you are dressed. What would you be wearing that would make you feel good?

How do you look for beauty in yourself and others?

Take yourself to a café and people watch for a while. Look at the people on the street and notice how they reflect their self to the world, paying close attention to the colours and shapes they are wearing. Sketch the outfits you like the most or write a list of the styles you want to explore.

- **What do you think are their best features?**

- **What do you see that reminds you of your own best features?**

- **How do you see others holding themselves, projecting themselves to the world, telling their own stories through their appearance?**

- **What can you learn from this?**

Consider how you might choose to present yourself to the world, and what best suits your body and lifestyle. Write down your ideas about the look and feel you want to create.

- **What message do you want to give others about you from the way you dress?**

Fake it until you make it

If you were born without wings, do nothing to prevent them from growing. Coco Chanel

So you don't feel confident, empowered or sexy today? One of the easiest ways to bring on these feelings is to dress as though you already feel it.

While it's normal and natural to compare ourselves to the media images we are surrounded by every day, remember that these are unrealistic, uncommon and often retouched. These images serve the economy and advertisers well but do not reflect reality or help us feel good about ourselves. Try to suspend all comparisons. Imagine seeing yourself the way someone who loves you deeply would see you. Appreciate your body and notice what you like about it. No matter how you feel, dress up and show up — you may surprise yourself.

Dress as though you feel successful, strong, attractive and, believe it or not, you *will* start to feel it. It's difficult to feel frumpy in a kick-arse suit or fabulous frock. And when people respond to you *as though* you are successful, confident and strong, your self-image is reinforced and the outcome can only be great.

Keeping yourself well groomed and looking after yourself is a great confidence-booster because it's a way of saying, 'I'm important.' Even before you put on a thread of clothing, treat yourself with feel-good body pampering treatments — see the tips for a day spa at home later in this section. Once you are feeling good underneath, dress for success and notice how energised you feel. Hold your head up and give your clothes a chance to sit on your body well. Pulling your shoulders back does wonders for making yourself look well groomed. Focus on your good bits and keep enhancing them. Get better at graciously accepting those compliments — there'll be many more to come!

What do you notice about yourself when you feel confident? What might others notice?

When you feel confident, how do you dress?

What kind of make-up could help you increase your confidence?

What outfits do you wear that attract compliments?

How would you feel about receiving more compliments in the future? What difference would it make? How would your posture and body language change?

If you dressed for the job you want, rather than the job you have, what would be different?

Sort out
your wardrobe

I have always believed that fashion was not made only to make women more beautiful, but also to reassure them, give them confidence. Yves Saint Laurent

In a busy lifestyle people can often get stuck wearing the same old thing. Maybe it's the old 'better the devil you know' attitude or a fear of experimenting with change. Fashion magazines make looking good seem terribly complicated and risky; it's much easier to stick with what is familiar. But how we project ourselves to the world has a strong reciprocal relationship with our self-confidence and happiness.

Just opening the wardrobe with the intention of sorting it out is a challenge for most of us! This is one of those activities where support and encouragement can really help. Is there a friend who could help you make decisions about those clothes that suit you and help you feel good, and those that should really be passed on to charity? Choose someone whose style you admire and who you can trust to be una-shamedly honest with you.

You'll probably want someone whose style is compatible with how you would like to look (but not necessarily the same). A punk rocker might not be equipped to give the best input on your corporate wardrobe. Blokes may wish to ask a female friend to help them, or a stylish gay friend always comes in handy.

If you're doing it alone, be kind to yourself, but be brave and bold: be prepared to challenge yourself and the mirror to achieve your best results. You know when you look and feel great. Listen to yourself and value your own opinions.

Begin by culling everything that isn't useful, beautiful or joyful. This means anything that is worn out, doesn't fit, or doesn't suit your shape or lifestyle. If you haven't worn it in more than a year, take that as a sign. Make sure you have a good full-length mirror; it's amazing how different some outfits look when you can completely see them. And when you look at yourself in the mirror, beware that negative self-talk.

Make piles of clothes: those to be mended, those to go to charity, those for the rubbish bin, and those too hard to get rid of (pack these away). Do the same with your underwear: make sure it fits properly and toss everything that is worn out. Only keep the clothes that make you look good and feel great. Go through your shoes, coats and accessories. You may discover that the quality of what remains lifts remarkably.

Consider the clothing you need for your lifestyle. Experiment with new combinations. Grab your journal or a notebook and write down these new combinations. You could also take a quick digital picture. Make some notes about things that you could update or that might add a finishing touch to your wardrobe.

Finally, store your clothes in a way that will help you in your daily routine and arrange them so they are easy to see and access, such as by colour or type. When clothes are organised, it's easier to choose an outfit and your mornings will become instantly less frantic and stressful.

Now that you have sorted out your wardrobe, consider what will help maintain it. Is it regularly doing your washing and ironing or keeping your accessories well organised and in good condition with a regular clean? Perhaps it is knowing good combinations in advance, or having your clothes stored in a way that makes them easier to access. Whatever it is, set yourself up to make the most of what you've got.

What could you do to spend less and have more to wear?

What is it that you can never find in your wardrobe that you need?

What would most help your mornings go more smoothly?

How can you organise your clothes so it makes dressing easier?

Dress to make yourself
feel good

The best colour in the whole world is the one that looks good on you. Coco Chanel

The next time you see someone walking along the street who looks fabulous, look carefully. Is it really because they're slim? Or is it that they dress well for their shape, in colours and styles that make the most of what they've got?

Do yourself a real favour by focusing more on your shape than your size when you dress. By honestly and accurately assessing your body shape, you'll come to understand how you can emphasise the good bits and disguise the not-so-good bits.

Length is one of the most important factors to consider when deciding what suits your figure. Compare short-, medium- and longer-length tops and bottoms. Fitted is more flattering than either loose or tight, both of which can make you look bigger than you are. If the shape doesn't suit you, don't buy something just because it's fashionable.

Colours can dramatically affect the way we see the world and how we feel about it. Colours both reflect and generate feelings and sensations. And how you respond to colours is also an entirely subjective experience: what suits you is highly individual. You can work out which colours suit you by holding different hues near your face. Some colours will make you look healthy and vibrant, while others will make you look like you are at the wrong end of a big night out. Fashionable colours come and go, so it is important to know what core colours work for you. It makes shopping that much easier, too.

Black may be safe, but it's not always slimming — it can make some bodies look heavier because there is less opportunity to break up the whole into different shapes.

As you grow in confidence and try new options and colour combinations, new favourites will emerge. They'll be colours that make you feel happier, more optimistic and better about yourself. Try wearing something bolder than you usually do and see how it affects your day.

As we get older, another challenge emerges: what sorts of clothes look best at our age? If you're young, you can get away with wearing a wide variety of styles. It's a period of fun and experimentation, so you might as well enjoy it.

Most people in their thirties and forties have started responding less to the whims of fashion and more to their own sense of style. By the time salespeople start referring to you as 'mature', you might find that comfort and practicality are new priorities. There's an emphasis on tailoring and better quality, but also for looking at ways to keep the classic styles interesting, especially through colour and accessories.

Young, middle aged or older — be proud of the stage of life you are in by dressing to celebrate it.

What do you wear that makes you feel good about yourself and happy about your life?

Which styles best suit your shape?

What colours match your personality? Which tones make your face light up and eyes sparkle? Which colours suit your skin tone?

What clothes best suit someone in your age group?

Allow your personality to shine

Find ecstasy in life; the mere sense of living is joy enough. Emily Dickinson

Accessories are a fantastic way to update your wardrobe. A feature piece of jewellery can lift a whole outfit. Add a stylish scarf, cute hat, quirky antique brooch or bright handbag to an old outfit and suddenly it's new again. Well-placed accessories can also distract attention from the bits you are not feeling so happy with.

Accessories help you create an individual look and, because they don't have to be expensive, they make it easier to follow some trends without being a slave to fashion. Animal prints are in? Forget the pants and buy a scarf instead. Go for cheap and cheerful when it comes to the latest trends, otherwise invest in quality pieces. A plastic bangle (perhaps a vintage one) may not cost the earth but will give your outfit a lift. Coco Chanel combined real and costume pieces, so you can too.

Eyeglasses come in all shapes, sizes and colours and they make a statement about who you are. Are you wearing the same frames you've worn for the past fifteen years? A new pair of stylish glasses can instantly transform your look. Choose a style that suits your colouring and facial features. Sunglasses can give an outfit an instant fashion lift and are a good way to camouflage age lines. Of course, they also protect your eyes from sun damage.

For men, simple touches such as a good watch, funky hat or sunglasses can individualise an outfit and make you stand out from the crowd. Choose accessories that say something about your personality. A great watch or tie is an investment that cannot be overvalued. Old-style hats, both winter and summer, can be very dashing. A special scent can be uplifting, but when it comes to men's cologne buy quality and wear it sparingly. Cufflinks, scarves and beanies can all allow your personality to shine.

People often notice accessories and comment on them. Choose pieces that are meaningful or that symbolise something important to you: they become a talking point. Aim for the wow factor and have fun.

How can you update your wardrobe?

What accessories work best for you?

What kind of look do you want to create?

INSPIRING IDEA

Try dressing like your favourite movie star or styling your look to suit a certain era in fashion. Making a new look is also about combining different styles and traditions and putting them together differently.

Pamper yourself

*And forget not that the earth delights to feel your bare feet
and the winds long to play with your hair.* Khalil Gibran

Most people are at their best when rested, relaxed and feeling good. Lavish day spas are many people's idea of a day of happiness. Although this happiness may be short-term, a day-spa experience can be a great way to pamper and re-energise your body, slow down your mind, and make some space for quiet contemplation. You emerge glowing and feeling healthy.

Create your own day-spa experience at home. There is something wonderfully restorative about treating yourself to a soothing hot bath. At the end of the week, or when you feel you need some pampering, a hot bath can be a wonderful way to spend time alone or with your partner (assuming you can both fit, given modern-day baths seem to be shrinking!).

Ideally, you'll have the house to yourself but that's not always possible. Work with what you've got. First, set the mood with relaxing music, candles or essential oils in an oil burner. Fill the bath, adding bath salts or oil. Exfoliate using a body scrub with a beautiful vanilla, rose or frangipani fragrance, rubbing it over the skin using circular movements. You can use exfoliating gloves to invigorate the skin. A deep-conditioning hair treatment can add extra softness, especially for dry hair.

Sip herbal tea throughout your day-spa experience to keep hydrated — make a refreshing tea by adding a few mint leaves and fresh lemongrass to a pot of hot water.

Or you could indulge in a glass of champagne.

To complete your day-spa experience, apply some luscious moisturising cream to keep your skin hydrated and feeling wonderful.

How can you create your own indulgent pampering experience?

What routines help your skin, hair and nails feel well cared for and rejuvenated?

My commitment to dressing and grooming

What I like about the way I currently present myself is:

My goals for improving how I present myself are:

These things have worked for me in the past:

Other sources of support and encouragement I can use are:

I can boost my confidence by:

My next step is to:

DOMAIN 3:
Designing your living space

Have nothing in your house that you do not know to be useful, or believe to be beautiful. William Morris

Many people's favourite space is their home. It's the place where you can be yourself with those closest to you. A home can also be an expression of who you are.

Recently some friends prepared their home for sale. They got rid of the clutter, and fixed what was damaged, then painted and styled their home. The transformation was so amazing they did not want to leave. Another thing they noticed was how much easier it was to keep the house clean. They said, 'If only we had done this earlier we could have enjoyed it so much more.'

Whether you prefer the simplicity of uncluttered spaces or the richness of plentiful ones, an overhaul of your living space, garden or workspace can help you refocus. Consider what inspires you about your surroundings and what might enrich your life. Enhance your day-to-day happiness by filling your home with items that have special meaning for you, such as travel mementos or photographs.

Take a slow stroll through your home, listening carefully to your inner promptings. Stop in each room and notice ... where do you feel most comfortable?

What helps you feel comfortable?

Where do you feel a sense of happiness?

What exactly is it about each of those spots that helps happiness flow in you?

What does this tell you about the styles and themes that you like?

Who else lives in this space and what are their preferences?

CREATIVE CHALLENGE

Collect pictures of houses you like, take photographs of colour schemes that catch your eye, collect pictures of accessories that appeal. Paste them into a visual journal as a collection of ideas about the look and feel you want to create in your home.

What do you notice about the themes or patterns that run through the pictures you collected?

- **How can you use these ideas to improve your current home?**

De-clutter

Live simply so that others may simply live. Saint Elizabeth Ann Seton

Many people find that clutter detracts from the look of a home while clear space enhances it. A less cluttered room appears more spacious and is easier to clean, making housework less onerous.

Start with clearing out your storage areas (cupboards, sheds, garages) and keep only the things you use regularly. Chances are you will have forgotten much of what you keep in there. Once you have more space in your storage area you can use it to de-clutter other areas.

Take an hour or so to de-clutter a room. Look for all the things that are not really needed or noticed. Remove the item or find a better place for it. When getting rid of clutter, ask yourself: Do I really need this? If I didn't have it anymore when would I be inconvenienced? When was the last time I used this? Could someone else benefit from this more than me? Does this stuff take me closer to the life I want?

If you find it hard to part with things, or you and someone else disagree about getting rid of something, try putting items in storage for a while (chances are you will realise you don't miss any of them).

Baskets and boxes can be a great way to hide mess. Consider modern styles from homeware shops or go retro and pick up an old hat box or suitcase from an opportunity shop or antique store. Baskets and boxes create a contained and tidy look and help you keep track of things. It's very easy to do this with children's toys: storage buckets create order where once there was chaos. Mess is not really mess once it is in a box with a lid.

Another strategy can be to decide to reduce the amount of stuff in a room, a bag or a box by, say, half. Then if this is not enough, you could perhaps halve again. Simply sort the stuff into two piles: 'good' and 'less good'.

What do you do with the things you don't want anymore? Give the stuff away to friends or a charity shop. Giving something you really don't need to someone who does need it is not only generous, it's good for the environment. Hold a garage sale or sell valuable things online. The money you make can help finance other changes.

Lastly, avoid buying things you don't need. When shopping, ask yourself: 'Does this help me create the atmosphere I want in my home or will it just create more clutter?' and 'Can I save money and consume less?'

What spaces in your home can you simplify and make more spacious?

INSPIRING IDEA

Try not buying anything except food and essentials for the next month. Pay attention to how much you save and also to what you truly feel deprived of.

Create a **positive** living space

Your house is your larger body. It grows in the sun and sleeps in the stillness of the night; and is not dreamless. Khalil Gibran

Imagine a home that supports and nurtures your happiness. Picture it in detail: what kind of furniture, fixtures, textiles and colours does it have?

What changes can you make, however small, to the home you have right now to bring your ideal home into being right now? It's time to begin to create a home in which your happiness can flourish.

Start with a corner, a few shelves, one artwork, or a wall painted a colour that brings a smile to your face each time you see it. Look carefully at the flow of your home (how you move between spaces) and how the furniture is arranged. Making spaces special might initially include some cleaning, de-cluttering and rearranging.

Accessories such as a ceramic bowl, lamp, an antique, unusual artefacts or beautiful cushions can help you create your signature look. Pillows, rugs or textiles can help add texture and create an ambience that makes you feel happy. Art, especially a feature piece, can transform a room. A painting from a local artist need not cost the earth, and investing in art can also be a way of supporting artists in your community. Consider framing children's artworks or family photographs in modern or antique frames and hanging them together in a group.

Think about what anchors the room: where is the focal point? A feature piece creates interest, especially in the areas people see first, including the front yard, front steps, entrance door and hallway. Consider the best place in your home for a signature feature.

Next consider light and space. The right lighting can enhance darker rooms. Mirrors can create a sense of space by reflecting the available light. Let the sunshine in by raising the blinds. Open the windows and experience the flow of fresh air.

Aim for a coordinated, rather than matching, look. Personalise the space. Matching the style of your home to its era of architecture is not necessary. A mismatch of styles, such as modern furniture in an older style house, can create interest.

Create a home in which you can be authentically you and you will help create your own happiness.

What five words describe the space you'd like to live in?

What are the possibilities for transforming your current home to highlight some of the things that bring happiness into your life?

Which spaces in your home could you put to better use?

How can you improve your living situation without necessarily spending a lot of money?

What is your vision for the spaces you have?

Clean and tidy **as you go**

Simplicity is the ultimate sophistication. Leonardo da Vinci

Being able to relax in a clean house is many people's idea of pleasure. Keeping a stress-free, clean house can be achieved by getting into the habit of cleaning and tidying as you go.

How much extra effort is it to put your plates in the dishwasher, rather than the sink? It saves time to just put your laundry straight into the basket, rather than having to pick it up later off the floor. Fold jumpers and hang jackets as soon as you take them off. Use a valet stand for clothes you can get another wear out of. Make your bed as you get ready in the morning. Don't let clutter pile up — use storage boxes for things like kids' toys and shoes that are commonly strewn all over the floor. Better still, teach children to put their things away. Try to tidy before you go to bed or before you leave the house. Doing these things along the way helps to save a lot of time later.

Find a strategy that works with the people you live with. Have an agreed idea about where things belong so everyone knows where to return them after use and where to find them again later.

Apply the 'clean and tidy as you go' approach to larger jobs. My mother gives the house a general clean each week and focuses on one room each month for a more thorough clean. It's a plan that helps her manage 'spring cleaning' throughout the year, so it doesn't build up and become an enormous job.

How can you keep on top of small tasks so they don't build up to become large jobs?

Involve the whole family in looking after your home

Teamwork divides the task and multiplies the success. Anon.

Have you ever thought to yourself: 'I just want a clean home without arguments'? You don't need to be neurotic about cleaning, but developing a cleaning plan can help get you and your family into a routine and ensure an equitable workload.

Make use of the power of the collective. Decide on a few 15- to 20-minute time slots across the week (or one longer time slot for bigger tasks) when everyone does some of the household jobs. It is amazing what can be accomplished in a small space of time, and how equitable the workload feels when everyone is doing the chores at the same time. And consider re-distributing who does what once a month or once a quarter, so everyone gets skilled at all tasks, and nobody ends up doing a hated task without any respite.

With an agreed plan or routine, you can just get on with the job without having to think about it too much. And everyone knows what is expected of them, avoiding potential arguments. Giving children household chores gives them an opportunity to learn household-management skills. Perhaps incentives can be built in to keep everyone motivated. Remember, praise is one of the best rewards; nagging rarely provides an incentive.

Who enjoys doing which tasks?

Which are the tasks that no one wants to do? How might these be fairly distributed and cycled between people?

What does a cooperative household mean to you? How can it be achieved in practice?

How can you work together more effectively?

Create a garden
that brings positivity
to your life

It is not the language of painters but the language of nature which one should listen to. Vincent van Gogh

A garden can be a positive space in which you find peace and comfort. Some like their garden with nooks and paths that offer adventure, while others want a designer look with lots of open space. One of my friends gains much pleasure from gardening. Tending to her garden is a daily source of joy and relaxation. For others, gardening is one more chore on the list. What kind of garden will meet your needs?

Before you set out to improve your garden, first clean out the garden space. Prune and mow the lawn including trimming the edges. Remove the weeds and get rid of the rubbish. If you can, create a compost heap to add valuable nutrients to your garden soil.

Do you want natives, an edible garden, flowers or something low maintenance, such as succulents? Does your garden need to withstand a boisterous puppy or an energetic and curious toddler? Do you want to be able to entertain or are you just keen for some green?

How much time will you spend maintaining your garden? This will influence your choice of plants and the design of your space. Visit a local garden centre and take note of the plants you like or think would be suitable.

Community gardens can be great options for people with no backyard. People love the opportunity to get their hands into the soil and be 'earthy'. A community garden not only connects you with the environment, but is also a great way to get to know local people.

If you need extra help, consult a landscape designer or horticulture expert who has knowledge of design principles, plants and environmental management. They can help you make the best use of your land, creating a beautiful, practical and happy space to nurture your wellbeing.

What kind of garden will bring you and your family the most pleasure?

What features does your garden need to make it a happy place?

If you live in a home without a garden, how important is it to you to create an indoor garden?

Simplify
your workspace

Three Rules of Work: Out of clutter find simplicity; from discord find harmony; in the middle of difficulty lies opportunity. Albert Einstein

Our workspace says a lot about how we approach work and how organised we are. Being organised can help you cope better with stress in the workplace. When I'm feeling overwhelmed, the first step I take is to tidy my desk. It helps me to calmly focus on figuring out the most important things I need to do.

How our workspace is organised also sends messages about us to our colleagues and clients about how we go about our work.

Is the space where you work energising and motivating? Imagine yourself in your preferred workspace and how it might feel to work there. Create the kind of atmosphere that makes your workspace a pleasant place to be by adding plants, a fruit bowl, pictures, flowers, or items that have meaning for you. A teapot, coffee machine or plunger, and a selection of special teas can make having a break more special. Perhaps even rearrange the furniture.

As we spend more of our working lives online, think about how your work is organised in cyberspace. Have strategies to stay on top of email and for sorting files that make staying in control of your work easier and less stressful.

What would help to create the kind of atmosphere you prefer at work?

How can you cut down on clutter?

What systems do you need to keep you organised at work?

What would help to reduce stress or worry?

How do you use technology to help things flow more smoothly?

My commitment for improving my living space

The things I currently like about my living spaces are:

My goals for improving my living spaces are:

I created living spaces I liked in the past by:

Sources of support and encouragement are:

I can boost my confidence by:

My next step is to:

DOMAIN 4:
Promoting health and wellbeing

If we could give every individual the right amount of nourishment and exercise, not too little and not too much, we would have found the safest way to health. Hippocrates

Health is not just avoiding sickness. In positive terms, health is the capacity to grow to our full mental, physical and emotional potential — and to flourish. Being healthy is about feeling good and functioning well.

While many of us enjoy good health, there is also cause for concern. Our lifestyles need improving and our communities need strengthening. Many people do not eat enough vegetables or fruit, nor get enough physical activity.[11] There are increasing numbers of people who are overweight, while eating disorders are also on the rise.

Being healthy includes having a mind and spirit that is nourished and resilient. Yet more and more members of our community experience depression, anxiety or problems from drugs and alcohol. Mental-health issues affect one-third of families.[12] And, every 40 seconds, someone in the world dies of suicide.[13]

Most adults with mental-health problems first experienced issues as a teenager. Young people with a mental-health issue are also more likely to have low incomes, be in trouble with the law, be a parent, experience physical illness and have poor educational outcomes.[9] Tragically, suicide is one of the leading causes of death in young people.

Yet there is much reason for hope: conditions including anxiety and depression are treatable (although only a quarter of people affected seek help). Our understanding of mental illness is growing all the time. Suicide is preventable. And, even better news, we can promote good mental health to prevent problems.

Our health is largely influenced by our lifestyle and the environment we live in. If we are to focus on wellbeing rather than only treating illness, we must take responsibility for our own health rather than expecting doctors to pick up the pieces of our unhealthy lifestyles. It also means helping to make our community a healthier place in which to live.

The causes of chronic illness such as heart disease and cancer are mostly related to alcohol use, smoking, being overweight, not eating enough fruit and vegetables and physical inactivity.

Don't wait for a wake-up call. Our lifestyle is in our control: many of the illnesses we experience are preventable.[14] We need to build the strength of our minds and bodies so we are more resilient, making it less likely that problems will occur. And when we are in touch with our health and we know our bodies and minds well, we can catch problems early.

The healthier we are in body and mind, the happier we can be because, not only do we feel good, we're also more able to do the things that increase wellbeing. Researchers have also confirmed that there is a connection between happiness, health and life expectancy.[15] Put simply, healthiness affects happiness and happiness affects health.

What healthy habits do you already have in your life?

What does a healthy lifestyle mean to you?

How can you build healthy activities into a routine?

What would your partner or family wish for you in how you care for yourself?

(CREATIVE CHALLENGE)

Make an artwork describing what a healthy lifestyle would look like for you. Think about what being healthy means to you, what you are currently doing well, and what you need to do more of.

Bounce back

Happiness is a choice that requires effort at times. Aeschylus

No one is 100 per cent happy — if they were, there'd probably be a psychiatric diagnosis for it! George Bernard Shaw said, 'A lifetime of happiness! No man alive could bear it: it would be hell on earth.'

Negative emotions are not bad in themselves; it's what we do with them and how we think about them that are important. Happiness is about living an authentic life, which includes a range of emotions. Carl Jung said, 'The word "happiness" would lose its meaning if it were not balanced by sadness.' The key is creating a lifestyle that promotes being generally happier, not being on a continuous high.

Feeling sad or blue happens to everyone, but fortunately the feelings don't stick around. It's natural and normal to feel sad about things now and then. Within a few hours or days, the clouds lift and life looks more balanced again.

Depression, however, can hang around longer. Feelings of depression can come out of nowhere or they may be triggered by an event. The death of a loved one, for example, can have a huge emotional impact that lasts for some time. It's important not to feel ashamed or guilty about your emotions. Depression is not caused by weakness or failure. Know that when these feelings threaten to stick around and outstay their welcome, there are ways to show depression the door.

If you are depressed try to focus on small things you can do to move towards being healthier, even if you are not sure they will work. Build a walk into your day, talk to others, make sure you get out of bed early and into the morning light to keep a good sleep–wake routine. Plan your day, including some things you enjoy, reflecting on what makes them enjoyable. Mindfulness and being in the moment can be very helpful. Focus on the positive, no matter how small.

Most importantly, know that it's okay to ask for help. Talking to a health professional can make a difference. Try to keep your connection with friends, family and the community. Remember that these feelings will pass.

What have you learned from your friends and family about what's important when you're coping with a tough time?

Who supports you? Who helps you feel that you're not alone?

What daily activities help to bring some enjoyment to your day?

What helps you to bounce back?

Manage challenges

You are braver than you believe, stronger than you seem, and smarter than you think. AA Milne *in* Winnie-the-Pooh

People's resilience never ceases to amaze me. The way people are able to reach out to others, how they laugh at themselves, and how they find the ability to put their lives together again after experiencing a tough time is resilience.

Resilience comes from within and gives us a sense of control over our lives, the ability to solve problems and to persevere. It also allows us to continue to build connections with others. Our resilience is also built by external forces, through our social supports and our sense of belonging within the community. Resilience is something we all have and use day-to-day, not just something we use to help us bounce back from life's knocks.

Coping with life's challenges can be especially tough when things do not go as we had hoped. Everyone experiences challenges — our feelings of happiness fluctuate. Difficult life events can happen to anyone — being retrenched, having an accident, losing a loved one — and we need to respond to adversity as best we can.

Think about a difficulty or life experience, big or small, that was a challenge. How did you manage? What helped you cope?

When we come up against something unexpected, one of the most effective management strategies is to create a picture of the future without this challenge. Take some time to imagine: what will be different? How will you know when the problem has gone? How will you feel about yourself? Then, identify the first step to making that picture real. Remember to think about what you are most looking forward to about getting through this challenge. How will you celebrate when it's resolved?

Sometimes, you may not be able to change your circumstances. There's great wisdom in accepting that there are some things you cannot change. Even so, if you can't change the circumstances, you can change how you think about them. Try to find opportunities in life's challenges. Many people have become more grounded, centred, connected to others — and happier people in the process — despite tragedy.

What tells you that you are coping well?

What strengths and resources do you have that will help you?

When have there been times that these challenges did not affect you as much?

What's different when things are going better? What do other people see you doing?

How would you explain your ability to do things differently then?

Eat well

When you do things from your soul, you feel a river
moving in you, a joy. Rumi

If 'we are what we eat', then let's aspire to be healthy, moderately sized, colourful, fresh, diverse and tasty.

Enjoy the feeling of being good to your body. Relish the feelings of health, strength and positivity when you eat well rather than resentfully chomping on mournful celery. We can start making conscious choices about what we really enjoy eating, rather than using food as punishment or a means of rebellion. How often have you rebelled by eating something 'naughty' then realised you didn't enjoy it? When we start listening to what our bodies really want and enjoy, we find that our diet becomes an integral part of our self-respect.

Know what you are eating by reading the labels on food packaging, paying close attention to the total energy, fat and salt content. The World Health Organization recommends that we limit the consumption of unhealthy fats (shifting away from saturated fats to unsaturated fats and eliminating trans-fatty acids); limit sugars and salt; and increase our intake of fruits, vegetables, legumes, wholegrains and nuts.[16]

Sometimes the most enjoyable part of the food is not in the eating, but the sense of achievement you get from cooking and preparing something delicious that is appreciated by others. Trying new foods and dishes, especially freshly prepared meals, can bring enormous pleasure. Explore new flavours such as fresh herbs, chillies, garlic and balsamic vinegar, and adapt old recipes to make them healthier.

Have a good breakfast to kick-start your metabolism for the day. Eat the recommended serves of vegetables and fruit per day (this usually means eating more not less!). Having a vegetable soup for dinner can be a great winter warmer and is an easy way to increase your veggie intake. A refreshing salad in summer can serve the same purpose — take a lesson from the Europeans who have a salad as their first course.

Remove temptation and don't have junk food in the house. We all have moments of weakness; no one is perfect, so limit the potential damage. Choose healthy snacks, such as fruit, low-fat soups, a small handful of nuts, wholegrain crackers or air-popped popcorn, and have them nearby both at home and at work.

Aim to eat only moderately sized meals. One way to manage portion size is to plate your food before sitting at the table rather than having a buffet-style meal in front of you, ready for easy picking. Avoid reading or watching TV while you eat and instead, eat slowly and notice the flavours.

Look for healthier alternatives when eating out or buying takeaway. If in doubt, ask how the food is cooked — how many times have you imagined a lean grill and received an oily, fried dish instead? Choose an entree and a side dish instead of a main if the main course options don't suit. And share dessert — it's more fun and only half the kilojoules.

How does food bring happiness into your life?

How do you most enjoy sharing food with others?

What do you need to change about your daily eating preferences to improve your health?

What is important for you to remember when shopping for food?

Prepare a meal that stimulates all your senses and increases your enjoyment of food. Who will you invite to share this meal? What kinds of foods will you serve? What else would make the event special?

Choose water
as your drink

If there is magic on this planet, it is contained in water. Loren Eiseley

When models are asked for their top beauty tip, many of them say, 'Drink plenty of water.' Keeping hydrated not only helps you to manage your weight, but it also keeps your skin soft and supple.

Adults should drink 2 litres of water per day — that's eight glasses. Children should drink 1 litre — four glasses. Vary the quantity with the season and climate and remember, drinks with caffeine or alcohol don't count.

One of the biggest contributors to weight problems in children is sugary drinks. Many people don't realise a can of soft drink has 10 (or more) teaspoons of sugar — and no other nutrients! Would you put 10 teaspoons of sugar in your tea or coffee?

If you are a parent, set an example by drinking water yourself. Make water easily available by keeping cold water in the fridge, serve water with your meals and pack a drink bottle filled with water for school. Water can be made more interesting by adding ice cubes, using a straw or adding a slice of orange or lemon. Get into the habit of taking a bottle of water from home when you go out.

For children, milk is an important drink because it provides valuable nutrients, including calcium and protein. Older children should drink reduced-fat milk.

Children under two can drink full-fat milk because they have higher energy needs than older children.

Most fruit juices provide nutrients but contain little fibre, so, unfortunately, they don't give the same benefit as eating fresh fruit. Many fruit juices are also high in kilojoules and sugar, so like soft drinks they should only be consumed occasionally.

Drinking water regularly will not only set a good example to your children, it will help you manage your weight and boost your complexion too. If you struggle to drink eight glasses of water each day, try to drink a glass every time you start a new activity. Every time you walk past the sink, drink a glass of water. Every time you go to the toilet, drink a glass of water … You'll quickly find you're up to eight glasses without even trying.

Do you need to increase the amount of water you drink? If so, what will encourage you to increase your daily water intake? How will you keep track?

Switch off the screen and get active

Lack of activity destroys the good condition of every human being, while movement and methodical physical exercise save it and preserve it. Plato

Plato knew it more than 2000 years ago and researchers today have confirmed it: people who exercise regularly are happier.[10] While exercise can boost your mood and increase happiness, around 40 per cent of people worldwide do not get enough physical activity.[17]

As well as promoting psychological wellbeing, regular physical activity can help prevent lots of health problems. The World Health Organization says physical activity reduces the risk of cardiovascular disease, some cancers and type 2 diabetes. It can also improve musculoskeletal health, control body weight and reduce symptoms of depression.[14]

Time spent in front of the TV or at the computer contributes to weight problems, particularly in children. Children and young people should spend less than two hours a day sitting in front of a screen.[18] Plan a range of indoor and outdoor activities with your kids as an alternative to watching TV or playing on the computer.

How much exercise do we need? Thirty minutes of moderate activity most days will do it. You can also combine a few shorter sessions of activity of around 15 minutes each. Moderate activity means you can still comfortably talk (but perhaps not sing)

while doing the exercise. If you want to take it to the next level, schedule some regular, vigorous activity for extra health and fitness.

Plan your exercise by adding it to your diary. Decide how many times each week you want to swim, go to the gym, take a yoga class, play tennis, or do whatever activity feels good for you. Then, schedule it just like you would a meeting or doctor's appointment. Use the healthy and happiness-making plan in Part 1 of this book to make a weekly exercise routine.

What kind of physical activity would fit well in your current routine?

What has worked in the past?

How does exercise boost your happiness?

INSPIRING IDEA

Go for a walk in your neighbourhood and find a path that increases your sense of happiness. While walking, think about what things make you happy and your journey to create greater happiness in your life.

Be active in as many ways as you can

Wholesome exercise in the free air, under the wide sky, is the best medicine for body and spirit. Sarah Louise Arnold

You are more likely to maintain regular activity in your daily life if you include exercise that is purposeful and part of what you do every day. Look for opportunities to exercise by walking instead of driving short distances. This is especially important if you already feel that life is jam-packed or if the thought of finding time for exercise is overwhelming.

Try taking the stairs instead of the elevator at work or go for a walk at lunchtime — it's a great way to de-stress from the office and spend time with a friend.

Your travel time is also a great way to build exercise into your routine. Try walking or cycling if that's something that appeals to you. You could get off the train or bus one stop early and walk the rest of the way. How about a walk before or after work? You could use it as a chance to catch up with your partner or children before or after a busy day.

Walking children to school helps them learn about 'normal' physical activity. It can help prevent weight problems and to connect with the community around them. The journey gives opportunities to meet others along the way and it's a good time to talk to your kids and keep communication pathways open.

Playing sport can be a fun way to exercise no matter your age or ability. Team sports are also an excellent way of meeting people with similar interests and broadening your circle of friends. Most sporting clubs arrange social events throughout the season. There are often opportunities to help with the running of the club.

Yoga and Pilates are associated with increased flexibility, strength and clarity or peace of mind. They can be a terrific adjunct to other sports or more vigorous activities. Many yoga devotees swear by it as a way of dealing with stress and calming their minds. Pilates uses coordinated breath and movement to strengthen and stretch the body, working on balance, posture and core strength. It's similar to yoga, but there's more emphasis on movement as each exercise is repeated. Pilates focuses on the deep abdominal muscles, buttocks, hips and lower back strength. It also improves balance, posture and flexibility.

Know what motivates you. Is it having a routine, exercising with a friend or group, or having a personal trainer? Having a routine involving friends or family members also makes it difficult to give up or back out. Maximise your success by using what keeps you motivated, interested and enjoying your workouts. If you're goal-oriented, set yourself a challenge: a local fun run can be something to work towards and help you maintain focus. Perhaps a dance or Zumba class is just what you need to bring a smile to your face and enliven your body? Whatever you choose, just keep moving!

What keeps you motivated when exercising?

What kinds of sports and physical activities do you enjoy?

Which ones would you like to try?

Limit alcohol

*One martini is all right. Two are too many,
and three are not enough.* James Thurber

An alcoholic beverage can be one of life's great pleasures. A glass of wine or a beer with friends can be a nice way to end the workday or to celebrate a big event. However, many of us also know how it feels to have had one (or three) too many. The key to enjoying alcohol is to keep the amount you consume to a level that doesn't impinge on your health and happiness.

Some people think, 'Well, I'm not an alcoholic, so I'm okay.' The truth is, drinking at harmful levels causes many health issues other than alcoholism: alcohol use contributes to cardiovascular disease, cirrhosis of the liver and various cancers. Alcohol weakens the immune system so often has a role in infectious diseases. Alcohol also plays a part in many injuries, both unintentional and intentional, including road traffic accidents, violence and suicide.[19]

Regular heavy drinking and binge drinking are dangerous to our health and happiness.[20] Limit your drinking to two standard drinks per day for women (a standard drink is 100 millilitres) and four for men, with at least one to two alcohol-free days each week. At a party or night out, aim to have no more than five standard drinks in one sitting.

Knowing how to count your drinks is important, especially when driving. Your size, weight, fitness, liver function and whether you are male or female will all affect the alcohol level in your blood and the rate at which alcohol is eliminated from your system. Another thing to remember is that some medications can increase the effects of alcohol.

Before an event, plan how much you are going to drink. Choose drinks that have less alcohol or dilute your drinks using mixers such as soda water. Experiment with creating luscious fruit cocktail combinations with little or no alcohol. Always start with a non-alcoholic drink and make every second drink a non-alcoholic one. I have a friend who, when out, makes sure everyone is armed with a glass of water. Have you ever noticed that people will often drink a glass of water given to them, even when they did not specifically request a glass?

If you are drinking a little too much or if drinking is causing problems in your life, it's time to act. Decide if you will go alcohol-free or limit your drinking to safe levels. Which approach is most likely to achieve a positive result for you? You can always change your mind anytime you think a different choice will increase the likelihood of a good outcome. See a drug and alcohol counsellor, psychologist or social worker, or talk to your doctor or a telephone support service.

What would a relative, friend, doctor, health worker or co-worker recommend about your drinking?

Do you want to reduce the amount you drink or do you feel you would be better not drinking at all? If you want to reduce your drinking, what are your specific goals?

What strategies will you use to help you stay motivated? How can you encourage yourself?

If you are using alcohol as a way of increasing your sense of happiness, what else can you use to create this same feeling without the risks involved with alcohol?

Quit smoking **for good**

To cease smoking is the easiest thing I ever did. I ought to know because I've done it a thousand times. Mark Twain

One of the best things you can do for your health is to stop smoking. One cigarette reduces your life by eleven minutes.[21] Because people are having children later in life, and because we know smoking cuts about ten years from your life,[22] choosing not to smoke can mean the difference between knowing your grandchildren or not.

Quitting smoking can be challenging, so be sure to get all the help you need. The first step is to be clear about the reason you're quitting. The strongest motivation lies in focusing on what you'll gain by quitting, rather than only focusing on the harm of continuing. Perhaps you want to quit because of the health risks, to find a new partner, or because you want to know your grandchildren.

It's very common to start the process of quitting while still wanting to smoke. This is normal. Don't put off quitting because you feel this way — there is lots of help to get you through. If you've tried to quit before, you can use what you learned about what worked last time — and what didn't help — to make your plan to quit stronger.

Next, explore options to help you quit smoking such as patches and quit-line services. Look for other supports such as friends who have quit or who also want to quit. Most importantly, set a date to quit and stick to it.

Now, put the plan into action. It's normal to get cravings in situations where you used to smoke. Resisting cravings is a necessary step in making them go away. Each time you exercise your willpower, your willpower grows stronger. If you do have a cigarette, you don't need to see it as a one-way-ticket back to full-time smoking. Be aware of risky times or situations and prepare a plan to help you manage.

The next stage is learning to enjoy and value your new smoke-free lifestyle. Start to think of yourself as a non-smoker. Give yourself a huge pat on the back!

How will you benefit from being a non-smoker? How will you remind yourself of your reasons for quitting?

What will be the signs that you are keeping your commitment to quitting?

What situations do you need to prepare for to make it less likely you will slip? How will you respond to urges to 'just have one quick one'? What strategies have worked best in the past?

Think of a time when you did something that was difficult and you nevertheless succeeded. How did you do that? Is there anything you did then that could help you now?

How will you congratulate yourself every time you beat the urge for a cigarette?

Be drug aware

*Keep your head clear. It doesn't matter how bright the path is
if your head is always cloudy.* Unknown

There is a complex link between drug use and happiness. Many people initially try drugs because of some of the pleasurable effects: increased alertness and sociability, and reduced anxiety or worry. Initially, they may think that drug use is an easy way to increase happiness.

For many young people, experimenting with recreational drugs is just part of the exploration and risk-taking that goes along with youth. The problem is that many experiment with drugs without knowing the potentially harmful effects and dangers — and these have a negative impact on their happiness. For example, taking cannabis can lead to dependency, an increased risk of motor-vehicle accidents, impaired respiratory function, cardiovascular disease and mental-health problems.[23]

Drugs can also cause relationship problems, money and legal problems and affect a person's ability to work and keep a job. There are also clear links between using drugs and mental-health problems: if you have a history of mental illness in your family, taking drugs may increase your risk of developing a mental illness.

For those who choose to use drugs, minimising harm is the key. Encourage young people to keep everyone as safe as possible. Teach them to look after friends who have been taking drugs. It's important that they keep hydrated and stay with their friend until the effects of the drug have completely worn off. If someone who has been taking drugs passes out or needs help, call an ambulance immediately. The paramedics are not required to notify police in the case of an overdose.

It is also wise to research the effects of different drugs and know what they do, physically and mentally. Be aware that mixing drugs, especially with alcohol, can be lethal. If you decide to use drugs, don't mix them. Take one drug at a time, use smaller amounts and don't forget that some drugs have a delayed effect. Consider whom you want to be with and where, in case you have a bad or unexpected reaction. Find someone to look after children so they are safe and are receiving the attention they need. Be aware of the potential dangers at parties and clubs, such as drink spiking — hold onto your drink and don't drink anything that's been out of your sight. Pre-plan how you will get home safely.

Parents of young people can help reduce the risks by educating them about how they can best manage risks and make a plan to stay safe. Most importantly, teach by example.

If you are worried or concerned about your drug use (recreational drugs and/or prescription medication) or about how drugs are affecting someone in your family, get help. Talk to your doctor or a drug information line and get the support you need to make changes in your life.

How can you protect and support those close to you who may be taking drugs?

What is the effect of your drug use and that of your friends and family on your relationships?

How does your and others' drug use affect your ability to care for others?

Manage other addictive habits

You cannot beat a roulette table unless you steal money from it. Albert Einstein

There are many other addictive habits that don't involve drugs — some damaging, and some not so damaging. Believe it or not, you can become addicted to exercise: not usually a problem, unless it begins to be harmful. Playing computer games or being online for long periods may also begin to interfere with your life if it replaces other activities that would make you ultimately happier, particularly as they are sedentary activities.

Gambling is another addictive activity that can cause significant problems for individuals and families. People often feel depressed, anxious or guilty after gambling — it's called a gambling hangover. They may hide their gambling and try desperately to win back losses or win money to pay their debts. Tips for controlling your urge to gamble include being honest with yourself about how much you are losing (keep a record) and only gambling if you can afford to lose the money. Do not have your credit card with you if you gamble.

Eating, shopping and sex addictions are other known non-drug addictions that can greatly affect people's lives. For all kinds of addictions, it can help to tell someone who cares about you — or telephone a counsellor.

Do you have any habits you would like to change?

How would you prefer things to be?

What knowledge and resources will help you?

Live a life less painful

The great art of life is sensation, to feel that we exist, even in pain. Lord Byron

Although people experience pain differently, it commonly causes much worry and distress.

Acute pain is associated with an injury. The reason for the pain is clear (such as a broken arm) and it has a predicable duration and outcome. Acute pain can often be resolved by treating the underlying cause and managing the pain symptoms. It's okay to take drugs for acute pain for a short period; the risk of becoming dependent is low.

Chronic pain continues after the injury has healed. Pain that persists can have a significant impact on wellbeing, affecting relationships, work and mental health. The mechanism for most forms of chronic pain is unknown, unless it stems from a condition such as arthritis or diabetes. Drug treatments may only partially relieve the symptoms of chronic pain, so use them carefully. Many people find that therapies that focus on daily living, including how people think about their pain, are helpful.[24] Health-care professionals often recommend exercise, psychological strategies and lifestyle changes rather than drugs or surgery to improve chronic pain and the ability to manage it.

Both acute and chronic pain can make daily living a challenge. Try to maintain a healthy lifestyle, managing your physical fitness, eating healthy foods and ensuring you get all the rest you need. For some people, getting sufficient exercise is made more challenging by pain. In this case, find a type of exercise that takes your condition into account.

You may need to deal with flare-ups: it is best to have a plan worked out that you can use during these times. Take steps to prevent or ease depression by knowing what works for you, including talking to friends or professionals. Avoid using other drugs or alcohol to manage persistent pain. Don't allow the pain to curtail your life more than necessary. Instead focus on finding fun and rewarding activities.

How do you practise being happy even when you are experiencing pain?

How can you maintain a sense of hopefulness while also managing pain?

Get a **good** night's sleep

Sometimes the most urgent and vital thing you can possibly do is take a complete rest. Ashleigh Brilliant

Having a regular sleep pattern is important for your overall functioning and wellbeing. Most adults require seven to eight hours' sleep every night. Teenagers and children require even longer — nine to ten hours. Many people do not get enough sleep, disrupting their ability to function well and make good decisions throughout the day.

Get into good sleep habits by establishing a soothing bedtime routine and go to bed at the same time each night. Don't engage in stimulating activities before bed, such as playing a competitive game. Similarly, stay clear of the computer just before bed — an activity such as reading is more relaxing.

Disturbed sleep is common, especially during times when you feel stressed or emotionally overwhelmed. Anxiety, restless replaying of the day's events and heightened emotions may significantly interfere with sleep. Shift work and having small children often causes sleep disturbances. And we live in a digital world and our evening activities often involve some kind of screen or mobile technology — a great disrupter of sleep.

Eliminate all foods or drinks that contain caffeine six hours before bedtime. Limit your use of alcohol and tobacco and don't go to bed too hungry or too full. You can try drinking a warm drink such as chamomile tea, a natural herb that aids relaxation, before sleep.

Make your environment conducive to sleep by reducing noise and light in the bedroom. Keep the temperature in the bedroom at a comfortable level. Cover your alarm clock so you don't keep looking at the time. Restrict activities in bed to those that help to induce sleep, such as reading a book or having sex.

If you are unable to go to sleep (or back to sleep) after fifteen minutes, get out of bed. Do something that is not too stimulating but changes your focus, like listening to music, reading, relaxation exercises or meditation. My favourite cure for insomnia is to look out the window at the stars. If you are worrying about things at bedtime, write them down so you can put them aside until the morning. They often appear different in the light of a new day.

Sleep problems often respond to a change in context. Try sleeping in another room, sleeping wrapped up in a blanket as if in a cocoon, or going to sleep with soothing music. It may sound unusual but try sleeping with your head at the foot of the bed to see if it helps — I've found that it does.

A regular sleep pattern is important. Practise going to bed and getting up at the same time each day, to keep a good sleep–wake routine. Exercise daily, preferably in the morning, and avoid exercise in the hours before bedtime. Increase your exposure to natural and bright light during the day and turn off electrical devices at night. Avoid daytime naps and try not to sleep in on the weekends for more than two to three hours later than your usual wake-up time because it upsets your body clock. No wonder we are at our worst on Monday mornings!

We all know we feel much better after a good night's sleep and that burning the midnight oil affects our alertness, concentration and memory, so prioritise sleep in your daily routine.

Are you getting the sleep you need?

What helps you to get a good night's sleep?

Protect your health

The greatest wealth is health. Virgil

Some people take better care of their car than their own body. You only have one body so protect yours by preventing health problems from developing.

Protect your skin and eyes from the sun with a hat, preferably with a wide brim that shades the face, neck and ears. Wear clothing that covers as much of the skin as possible, including the back of the neck, and wear sunglasses to protect your eyes. Avoid the sun between 10 a.m. and 3 p.m. — use the shade from trees, umbrellas, buildings or any type of canopy. Use sunscreen on parts of the body that cannot be protected easily, such as the back of the hands.

Stay sexually healthy and avoid being caught out in the heat of the moment. Get your contraception organised ahead of time. Condoms are the only contraceptive that protects you against infections. If you use a condom and a water-based lubricant every time you have sex you will have less chance of contracting HIV or other sexually trans-mitted diseases. Keep condoms in your purse or wallet (because you never know …).

Look after your smile — it's one of your best assets! Eat well, enjoy a wide variety of nutritious foods and limit sugary foods and drinks. Drink plenty of water. Clean your teeth at least twice a day after meals and floss daily. See your dentist each year for a check-up.

Immunisation can protect you against harmful infections that can cause seri-ous complications, including death. Immunisation uses the body's natural defence mechanism — the immune response — to build resistance to specific infections. If you have children, keep to the recommended immunisation schedule. And if you're travelling overseas, leave plenty of time for vaccinations before you go (some need to be administered well before your planned travel).

Another way to stay healthy is to identify the early signs of problems. By identifying little things that seem unusual, you could prevent an illness from occurring altogether or enable a complete cure.

Health checks can literally save your life. Women need to check their breasts every month. Familiarise yourself with the normal look and feel of your breasts and see a doctor immediately if you notice any unusual breast changes. Men need to get familiar with the usual level of lumpiness in their testes and see a doctor if they notice a change.

Check your skin every three months for changes. The more often you examine your skin, the more you will learn about it — what is normal for you and what has changed since the last time you looked.

By preventing health problems — or detecting them early — you can take proactive steps to protect your health and wellbeing and avoid illness.

What steps do you take to protect your health?

Are you accessing the health care you need?

How can you remember to have your dental and other check-ups?

My commitment for promoting my health and wellbeing

I am currently doing well in looking after my health and wellbeing by:

My goals for my health and wellbeing are:

These things have worked for me in the past:

Sources of support and encouragement I can use are:

I can boost my confidence by:

My next step is to:

DOMAIN 5:
Managing finances

Real happiness is cheap enough, yet how dearly we pay
for its counterfeit. Hosea Ballou

How important is money for happiness? When money buys a way out of homelessness, or you no longer have to worry about where your next meal is coming from, it's very important. For the world's poor, and those poor on our doorstep, a small income is of tremendous value.[25] For wealthy people, a little extra money doesn't make a lot of difference.

Many countries have, in real terms, become richer and on average people live longer. Despite these gains, we are not getting any happier overall. High living standards in many countries have meant most of us have ready access to healthy food, health care, clean water and stable housing. But beyond a certain point, increasing a country's wealth does not bring greater happiness.[26]

The 2012 United Nations' *World Happiness Report* says that although a strong Gross Domestic Product (GDP) is a valuable goal in achieving high standards of living, other things matter greatly.[12] It advises that a strong GDP should not be pursued to the loss of economic stability, where the poor and socially excluded suffer, ethical standards are compromised, or the environment is put at risk. The vibrancy of communities and the mental health of people are more important. Economic growth needs to be environmentally and socially sustainable.

So, should we pursue economic development when economic growth does little to increase our wellbeing and happiness? Certainly, the happiest countries in the world have high incomes, but they also have high social equality, trust and high-quality governance and these are the significant differences between those countries and countries that are less happy.

While GDP is the top priority of governments, polls consistently suggest individuals value other things more highly, such as family and security. Some governments have taken on the challenge of improving national happiness by boosting social systems, supporting cultural activities, and protecting the environment. Perhaps we should look as carefully at our levels of happiness as we do our levels of national debt. We could learn something from the country of Bhutan, which measures Gross National Happiness as an indicator of its wellbeing.

How would we measure Gross National Happiness? Gallup polls measure people's assessment of their quality of life in more than 150 countries.[27] In the polls from 2005 to 2011, people from Denmark, Finland, Norway, the Netherlands, Canada, Switzerland, Sweden, New Zealand, Australia and Ireland rated their quality of life highest. Some of the features of those countries that scored highly include good social support systems (enabled by high taxation levels), comparatively evenly distributed incomes and low crime rates.

Most people who live in developed countries can afford to have access to the basic things that we all need: education, a bed at night, nourishing food, safe transport and health care. By distributing our wealth more fairly we can achieve these things for all people.

There's a growing consensus that, on the whole, we place too much emphasis on economic growth at a cost to our quality of life. Modern Western culture equates happiness with pleasure, gratification and indulgence, but we know that quick fixes of pleasure distract us from the things that bring long-lasting happiness. Connecting with others, having goals that use our strengths and abilities, and committing ourselves to the wellbeing of ourselves and others are more important. Ultimately, fulfilling relationships and not the accumulation of assets, are the key to happiness and wellbeing.

Look for ways to find enjoyment without spending money and manage your finances so they are not a source of stress — for most families this will promote happiness more than a few extra dollars in the kitty.

What role does money play in your sense of happiness?

What role would you like money to play in your sense of overall wellbeing and security?

CREATIVE CHALLENGE

Make a collage of the best life you can create for yourself while staying within your current income. Pay attention to the simple low-cost pleasures that you currently enjoy, and think about how you can create even more space for these happiness-making activities in your daily life.

Rethink your relationship with money

If you realise that you have enough, you are truly rich. Lao Tzu

Think about all the things you really want to do. Now think about all the things that make you happy when you are doing them. How do your answers differ?

Most people are surprised to discover that there is a difference between what they desire (what they think will make them happy) and the things that actually bring them happiness. Consumerism promises happiness but, for two reasons, it can never deliver. First, we adapt to what we have and we always want more. Second, we experience the problem of comparison: when we compare ourselves to others we feel worse off. People who have won the lottery have been known to become happier, but only for a limited period.[4]

Many studies have found that our need to purchase and acquire things is not associated with increased happiness, but with more negative emotions such as dissatisfaction, depression, anxiety and anger. And those who make comparisons between their own income and that of others are less happy than those who don't see their relative income as particularly important.[9]

If we want to bring happiness into our lives, we would be better off to focus more on our feelings of competence and self-worth, our relationships with others and safety in the community. Quite simply, people who care less about money are happier.[9]

That's not to say we shouldn't manage our money carefully. Responsible spending and money management are a source of good living and can help us feel secure. Not managing your finances well can bring about stress and worry. Consider your spending and saving patterns, your needs and wants, and work out realistic priorities and longer-term goals. Making active choices about our finances is connected to what we prioritise as important in our lives.

Recently a friend's five-year-old daughter was shopping with her grandmother. Her grandmother asked her, 'What do you need at the shops?' Skipping along and holding her grandmother's hand, she replied, 'I don't *need* anything, Grandma, I just want lots of things.' Children can have such simple wisdom.

If you had to choose between earning more money and cutting back on work, which option would make you and your family happier?

When you picture a healthy and happy lifestyle, what kind of job and income do you need to support that lifestyle?

How much do you spend on 'wants' as opposed to 'needs'?

How much money do you really need to live on?

Which 'wants' are you prepared to cut back on?

Start a loose-change jar or a savings account in which you bank the savings from reducing your impulse buying or by finding a cheaper alternative. If you're giving up smoking or reducing your alcohol intake, think about putting aside the money you save by not buying cigarettes or alcohol. See the positive impact your changes have financially.

Simplify
your finances

After a visit to the beach, it's hard to believe that
we live in a material world. Pam Shaw

Money may not bring happiness, but it can be stressful if your finances are not managed well. Wondering which bill you can pay this week and which can wait, struggling to find enough money for unexpected car repairs, or having to sell belongings to finance daily life can cause immense stress and unhappiness. Work out a plan to simplify and get on top of your finances, once and for all.

Develop a realistic budget to cover your expenses, including some rewards. Plan for large annual expenses, such as car registration, by setting aside money each month to cover that cost. That way, when the expense comes due, you won't find yourself living on baked beans for a month to cover it.

Look for ways to organise your living based on relationships rather than cash. Borrow or rent equipment you might not need longer term or re-sell items you have bought but no longer need.

Don't let bills weigh you down. Develop a filing system with at least two files: one for papers that need attending to and another for those you want to store. Set up as many automatic payments and direct debits as you can; that way you can avoid late-payment fees and save yourself a lot of time, energy and stress running around paying bills.

Plan, too, for unexpected events. Many a person has been knocked around financially because of sudden unemployment or illness. Having a few months' salary tucked away can give you flexibility and a sense of reassurance that the unexpected will be a hiccup rather than a disaster. If you have an emergency savings account then you will never really have any emergencies.

If you want to save for a specific purpose (such as a holiday), plan for it. You might like to look back at the section on setting SMART goals to help you. Open a specific account that is just for that goal. On payday, transfer the amount you want to save into that account before you do anything else. It's much harder to save money if you try to save what's left at the end of the pay period.

Take charge of any debt you hold. Pay off the loan with the highest interest rate first and try to pay off your credit cards in full each month. It also pays to shop around: use websites to compare the costs and conditions for credit cards, loans, car and health insurance to find the best deal and make informed decisions.

If one of your goals is to own a home, you'll need some careful financial planning and a long-term vision. Don't rush in. You need to carefully research the housing market and your finance options. Don't over-extend yourself; consider your circumstances given the possibility of future interest rate rises or a change in personal circumstances. Once you have a mortgage, look at making payments fortnightly rather than monthly — and if your loan is flexible, pay a little more than you need to. Over the term of your loan it can save you a significant amount of interest.

If that all sounds a bit restrictive, remember to not skimp on fun. Many cultural events and activities are free. Visit your local library, where books, movies and music are free to borrow and even the internet is free to use. Botanic gardens are also beautiful places to visit for little or no cost. Galleries, museums, beaches and parks are great options for low-cost entertainment.

Explore different holiday ideas: think about camping, self-catering accommodation, house-swapping or visiting friends. Check out websites that offer last-minute deals, especially for classy hotels. Instead of an overseas holiday, think about somewhere closer to home: take time to discover the gems in your own backyard.

How can you simplify your finances?

How much money do you set aside for the things you, your children and your family need?

Are there ways you can free up some finances without causing hardship or more stress?

The good life,
simply

*Not what we have but what we enjoy, constitutes
our abundance.* Epicurus

So many pleasurable everyday activities, such as reading a good book, walking the dog, having a nap, making a pot of soup, having a cup of tea, gardening, doing a puzzle or crossword, or listening to music, are low-cost.

Some of the most enjoyable and relaxing activities are simple things such as a log fire, a hot bath, burning scented oils, clean sheets on the bed and warm towels in winter, listening to a cat purr, or eating a boiled egg and toast on a rainy morning. Julie Andrews in *The Sound of Music* sang, 'Raindrops on roses and whiskers on kittens; bright copper kettles and warm woollen mittens; brown paper packages tied up with strings; these are a few of my favourite things.'

Acts of warmth and kindness are free yet mean so much: an unexpected hug, sending a thank-you note, making a casserole for a friend, picking flowers as a gift, telling someone you love them, sending a special message, making a birthday or Valentine's Day card, visiting a neighbour or telephoning a friend deliver joy to both you and the recipient.

There are also little moments of joy in life's experiences during which we reflect on the absurd, like when we smile at a cartoon. Or we might find ourselves observing life's magic: stargazing, people-watching from a distance, watching the sunset or leaves fall, or a spider at work.

Some activities bring back fond memories of childhood: eating watermelon on a hot summer's day, building sandcastles, eating pancakes, the smell of hot cinnamon cake. It's never too late to be a kid again. Pillow fights, skipping stones across a river, blowing bubbles and riding a bicycle are childhood delights that can be enjoyed at any age.

Being in nature, walking along the beach, swimming in the ocean, watching butterflies, lying on the grass and looking for shapes in the clouds, can all enrich the soul. Or you can get out into the bush, drive through mountains, bushwalk, tell stories, make tea and damper, and stare into the embers of a dwindling campfire.

Children bring many opportunities for low-cost fun: a picnic, playing games in the park, organising a treasure hunt, eating ice cream, watching planes at the airport, baking, or reading books.

Free activities might include going to the local library, a community event such as a music performance, visiting a gallery or watching a sporting match. Happiness-making experiences are often found just around the corner, without the need to open your wallet.

What things do you enjoy doing that don't cost a lot of money?

How can you include more of these in your life?

Which simple low-cost pleasures appeal to you?

Give of yourself

You give but little when you give of your possessions.
It is when you give of yourself that you truly give. Khalil Gibran

Giving brings more happiness than receiving. In a study in which one group was given money to spend on themselves and another group was asked to spend it on others, which group do you think was happier at the end of the day?[9]

So many things we can give — a compliment, a smile and a friendly hello — are free yet highly valued. Presents, too, don't need to cost a great deal — a thoughtful gift is more meaningful. Some people just seem to have the knack of being able to choose the right gift without spending a lot of money. The key is to find a gift that has meaning — take note of the small things people say and be imaginative. For example, you could replace a cherished object that was lost or broken, give something to help your friend achieve a personal goal, or give something you can enjoy together (Scrabble, anyone?).

A handmade card or drawing can be a fabulous gift, particularly when it has been made by a child. A poem or song can be a gift whose value cannot be measured.

Small children often love simple presents such as a decorated cake, a ball, puppet, book, costume, chalk or a special outing. You could give the teenager in your life a handmade pass that says you'll pick them up from any place, anytime, no questions asked. An adult might appreciate an IOU note for a favour, a glass of champagne together watching the sunset, a personally chosen mixed-song list, homemade jam or pickles, chocolates, or a framed photograph.

Ethical gifts can include things such as donating livestock or equipment to a family or school from a developing country.

When it comes to romance, little things create meaning and make a moment more special, and they needn't cost much. Walk along a beach together, go for a moonlit walk, or drive to a scenic lookout at sunset. Hold hands. Have dinner at home with candles, napkins and the good china and glasses. Buy special chocolates to top off a great home-cooked meal. Play cards, read aloud, pretend there's a blackout. Play 'your song' and dance. Or for a relaxed night in, watch a movie you both like, drink hot cocoa and have a pillow fight in your pyjamas. Then make your partner breakfast in bed or get up early with them even when you don't have to. Go to a park, play on the swings and feed the ducks. Go roller-skating. Share a candlelit bath together.

How can you bring more romance into your life without increasing your spending?

What message do you want your gifts to convey?

What would that person really love to receive?

If you are on a tight budget, what can you give that does not involve buying something? Your time? Your skills? Your company?

Finish unfinished business

It is not in the stars to hold our destiny but in ourselves. William Shakespeare

Imagine you knew you had just a few weeks left to live. What would be your priorities? What things would you need to set right?

I recently sat in a doctor's waiting room holding my file with my blood-test results attached to the front — a mistake made by the receptionist, who should have handed these directly to the doctor. For a whole fifteen minutes, I was convinced the results indicated I had a life-threatening illness. Thankfully, they didn't, but the experience did make me think about my priorities.

Tidying up unfinished business can bring a sense of peace. You might want to get in touch with an old friend, return something you've borrowed or finish an uncompleted project. Perhaps you really need to sort out your tax affairs or get some legal papers in order.

For many, making a will is an important step in creating peace of mind, particularly if you need to plan for the future of people you care about. You can choose who will handle your affairs after you die: this person is your estate's executor. Let them know where your will is. If you've had your will drawn up by a solicitor, they will usually hold it at no charge for you. If you've used a do-it-yourself-kit, make sure your will is somewhere safe but easily accessible.

Remember that if your circumstances change significantly (you get married or divorced, have children, buy a house) you'll need to update your will. Review your will annually.

Another thing you might like to do is to talk with someone close to you about what should happen if you are seriously ill or incapacitated. Discuss organ donation and how you feel about medical treatment in the event of a serious accident or illness. While these things are not easy to discuss, they can make future decisions and discussions much easier.

Once unresolved things are set right and loose ends tied up, we can relax and be more at peace.

What arrangements have you made for your affairs to be dealt with after your death?

What arrangements would you like people to carry out on your behalf if you are seriously ill or injured?

What changes in your circumstances do you need to include in your update of your arrangements?

Make **aware** financial decisions

There are those who give with joy, and that joy is their reward. Khalil Gibran

If we are to redress some of the inequalities that many people experience, both globally and locally, we need to be more mindful of how we earn and spend our money.

The products we buy and use locally have an impact on people in other countries. Many of the goods we use are made or grown in developing countries. Sometimes, they've been made by workers who receive little pay or work in dangerous conditions. Sometimes, the producers use child labourers. Farmers who grow products such as coffee or cocoa may not have received a fair price for their products. The manufacturing processes used may have been environmentally damaging.

Today, we're in the fortunate position of being able to make good choices and use our knowledge to choose products that are produced ethically. We can support companies that use ethical labour, pay producers fair prices, and adhere to environmental standards. Help businesses across the world by buying fair-trade goods.

You can also consider making sustainable and ethical investments. Many financial groups offer investment options that avoid making money from harmful activities. Socially responsible businesses consider the full range of costs and benefits of their activities, not just profit. Choose a superannuation fund that specialises in sustainable and ethical investments, or select this as an investment option if available. And if it isn't available, lobby your fund to provide that option.

Tread lightly on the earth. Become more environmentally aware and reduce your carbon footprint. Consider where items are made and how far they have been transported. Try to buy locally produced products wherever possible.

Given that extra income is much more valuable to the poor than the wealthy, consider making a regular donation from your income to organisations that support the disadvantaged or advocate for sustainable development. Or donate that unexpected tax refund or small windfall.

There are also many creative ways for making giving more social, such as pooling funds with a group of friends and jointly deciding how to donate it, donating a prize (perhaps becoming a 'patron of the arts'), or sponsoring a local sporting group.

How can you become a more responsible consumer?

What do you want to teach your children about how to manage money? How do you do that?

My commitment to managing my finances

What's currently going well with my finances is:

My goals for improving my finances are:

What has worked for me in the past is to:

Other sources of support and encouragement I can use are:

I can boost my confidence and financial competence by:

Financial resources I could consult when I need them are:

My next step is to:

DOMAIN 6:
Engaging in work

Work is love made visible. Khalil Gibran

You may have heard the expression, 'True happiness comes when you do what you're most passionate about.' It seems to be true that when we do what we love, we feel happier and more content. Do you love what you do?

Many factors influence how much we value our work. Researchers have found that people most value high income, flexible working hours, promotional opportunities, job security, interesting work, being able to work independently, helping others, and being useful to society.[9] The underlying values that affect people at work include pride, generosity, caring and honesty.[28]

Although high income featured on that list, it's interesting to note that research has also found that increased pay can, in fact, decrease our performance at work, because the money becomes more important than things such as security, autonomy, workplace trust and independence. Satisfied workers are more likely to stay in their jobs and are more likely to be productive.

Take some time to reflect on your skills, interests and priorities. How well do they align with what you do for a living? Thinking carefully about these things and how aligning work and your passions can increase your happiness might inspire you to change careers, change workplaces, downsize or undertake further study.

A friend was feeling unfulfilled in her work. She wanted to use her skills in a way that was more meaningful. She was struggling to find an answer when a job came up that called on her skills in marketing to do meaningful research with multicultural and indigenous people. She's now worked happily in the field for more than twenty years.

Don't be afraid to dream. Find your passion and create your life based on it. Promise yourself that you'll follow your dream.

What are you passionate about? When are you most alive and happy?

What's most important about work to you?

What maintains your interest in work?

What have you done that you feel proud of?

What is the work you'd like to be remembered for?

CREATIVE CHALLENGE

Take a step into the future. Imagine you are coming to the end of your working life. What would you like to be remembered for? What was your greatest contribution over the course of your working life? What skills, qualities and abilities did you use well in your work?

Perhaps create a final CV or a speech that someone might give at your retirement function.

- **What do you discover while doing this creative challenge?**

- **What do you want to include in your work so you can create the working life you've depicted?**

Do not be too worried about what you think may or may not be possible. Stick with developing a picture rather than figuring out how to get there — that comes later!

Do what you love

If you love what you do, there are no difficult tasks,
only interesting ones. Vadim Kotelnikov

It's often said, 'Choose a job you love and you will never have to work a day in your life!' What kind of work would bring about the most satisfaction, regardless of how much you were paid?

What are you good at? What do you most look forward to doing? Think about the sort of activities that suit your skills and interests. Knowing these things, you can start to think about what job might best match your skills, interests and talents.

How does your work fit with your goals, your family needs and the bigger picture of the life you want to create? When you start looking at your career options, keep an eye out for positions that match your most important values, interests, personality style, skills and strengths.

Many people change careers throughout their lifetime. Sometimes interests change; priorities shift or the work market requires different skills. Faced with the decision of what is the best job for you right now, what would people who want the best for you and your family advise you to do?

Your work can help you achieve a sense of purpose if it involves activities that you enjoy and that help others at the same time. Doing what you love, and what helps you to connect positively with others, is ultimately more fulfilling than earning more. How could you contribute to making the world a better place?

What qualities, skills and attributes do you appreciate about yourself?

How does your work give you a sense of meaning?

If you knew you had only twelve months to live, what would you regret not having done?

What is your life's mission? What job best suits your goals?

What do you love doing?

Visualise a day
in your preferred job

*Three grand essentials to happiness in this life
are something to do, something to love, and
something to hope for.* Joseph Addison

Trying to imagine your ideal job — one that is meaningful and satisfying — can be tricky. Usually, the picture is vague and fuzzy around the edges. One way to bring the picture into focus is to visualise a day in your ideal job.

Let's begin by imagining how your day begins. What time do you wake? What do you wear? Are the clothes similar or different to your current work wardrobe?

Now it's time to get going. How do you get to work? How long does it take and how do you travel?

You arrive at work. What kind of organisation is it? What is valued most in this profession and why is this job important to you? What's your physical working environment like? Where will you have lunch?

Imagine how you spend your day: What kinds of tasks are you doing? How do you spend most of your time? Do you spend a lot of time with other people or do you work by yourself? What skills do you need? What are the working conditions like? Do you earn enough to live on and support those you care for? What are the hours like? And the leave benefits?

It's the end of the day. What time do you go home? How do you feel when you get home?

This exercise can help generate the enthusiasm and energy you need to make the shift. It might also help you decide if you really do want it. You might decide, instead, to improve your current work situation so it is more like your preferred job. There are ways to do that: could you drop to four days instead of five? Would a day a fortnight working from home help you feel happier or achieve your goals? Perhaps you could organise a secondment to a different area if you're looking to learn new skills.

What aspects of this imagined job make you feel most happy?

What inspires you about this job?

What would be the next step to working in your preferred job?

How can you create some of this in your current job?

Be inspired

How far that little candle throws his beams!
So shines a good deed in a weary world. William Shakespeare

Who inspires you at work? Who notices the good in you and how do they encourage you to be the best person you can be?

Mentors or coaches can have a significant impact on us and give us the support we need to grow. The person who inspires you the most might not be your boss. It could be a colleague whose effectiveness you admire; a more senior person who shows interest in your career development; or a person who has achieved something you want to achieve in your career — and done it with style. Great mentors and leaders have the ability to connect with others, are genuinely caring, and inspire people to change for the better.

When I look back over my working life, the people who have influenced and supported me most strongly were consistently positive and optimistic. They urged me to undertake extra study and apply for new opportunities — to dare to 'step up'. They were excited for me and proud of my achievements. And they taught by both words and actions.

Who inspires you at work?

What have they taught you about what is most important?

Who encourages you at work?

What attributes and qualities do your workmates notice in you?

What gives you confidence in yourself?

Keep learning

The more you know, the less you understand. Lao Tzu *in* Tao Te Ching

The funny thing about study is that the more we learn, the more we realise there is much to know. And although this gives us a greater appreciation of our own ignorance, hopefully it also makes us more open-minded and humble. Learning keeps you young and the mind alert. It can also be the source of inspiration and happiness. And an added benefit: the more you learn, the easier life is.

Have you done all the study you want to do? What would you like to learn more about? How would further study take you to where you want to go?

The concept of lifelong learning means staying engaged, moving forward, and doing things better beyond childhood and school. Learning is a way to polish your skills and learn new ones, to engage with others and get involved, and to make the most of what the world has to offer. Higher education also leads to more highly paid jobs and better job security. And studying 'just for the fun of it' can be an enriching experience, broadening your outlook on life.

Many workplaces encourage people to self-direct and take personal responsibility for their own leaning. This helps people keep up with the innovations and developments in their professional field. But it also means being proactive in identifying the new skills you need to develop and the new areas you want to explore in your professional life.

We learn every day from experience and mistakes, asking questions, observing life and reflecting, through reading, talking with other people and through formal training programs. A mentor or coach may also be a useful way to support your development.

It is wonderful to see people excited about learning, who seek opportunities beyond their comfort zone, who are inspired to take up life's challenges, set goals, get started and move forward. And once you understand the theory, put your knowledge into action. As Morpheus tells Neo in *The Matrix*, 'There's a difference between knowing the path, and walking the path.'

> **Has there been something you have always wanted to learn about but never got around to? How will you know when it's time to begin? What will help you to get going with it?**
>
> **What is your motivation for improving what you do? How will improving benefit you and others?**
>
> **What are the skills or qualifications you would need for your ideal job? How would you go about gaining these?**
>
> **What choices now will help you be where you want to be in five years' time?**
>
> **What can you do that will increase the likelihood of you getting the job you want?**

Consider
downsizing

It is not how much we have, but how much we enjoy,
that makes happiness. Charles Spurgeon

Have you ever thought to yourself, 'I feel stressed and overwhelmed. I really need to get my priorities straight'? Research shows that once you get to a certain level of income, extra money won't make you happier.[9] Sadly, many people sacrifice family for income and personal success. But we know that people who set goals relating to their family or helping others are happier than those who prioritise career and material success.[10]

Downsizing is a deliberate choice made by people who are well into their career and can afford to sacrifice some of their financial position in order to gain a better quality of life. You may know people who've taken a sea change or a tree change.

It's becoming more and more common these days. People are choosing to downsize even though it means they earn less money. They may want to spend more time with family, live a healthier lifestyle, find a better balance or more fulfilment in how they spend their day, or lead a less materialistic and more environmentally friendly life.

You could think about working part-time, job sharing or starting your own business. What about early retirement, volunteering or working in the not-for-profit sector? Your version of downsizing might be about going back to university, taking over the child-rearing and housekeeping duties so your spouse can go back to work, following your dream of writing a book or travelling, or simply taking time off to re-evaluate your life.

Can you afford to work less?

Do you prefer the lifestyle that city or country life brings?

How does city happiness differ from country happiness for you?

If you were to change where you live, what might be the benefits?

Most change involves hard work. What hard work would such a lifestyle change require from you?

Let your workmates know what you appreciate about them

Kind words do not cost much. Yet they accomplish much. Blaise Pascal

How well does your workplace promote happiness and wellbeing? Take a moment to consider the relationship you have with your colleagues, and if you are a manager, those you support. Do your relationships at work support your happiness and that of others?

Often, it's everyday interactions that are the most meaningful at work. Positive workplaces welcome new employees and show respect, regardless of position. They are spaces where you can hear laughter. Workmates can have a good time together and people feel they can be themselves. Each person is valued for what they bring to the team.

Good relationships with the people you work with can ease your way through tough times. Humour strengthens positive relationships and can be a good way to cope with anxiety and stress at work. It also helps us make light of some of the problems we face.[4]

It's important to have fun every now and again. Make regular activities such as meetings, positive and productive and, whenever possible, try to make your workplace fun. One workplace I know of celebrates Chinese New Year each year with paper lanterns throughout the office and a yum-cha lunch.

Happy teams support and express their appreciation of each other. Try this: find a way to compliment every person you speak to — it will not only brighten their day, it will lift your spirits too.

How do you show appreciation to one another at work?

How do you survive in the tough times?

How do you show your workmates you care for their wellbeing?

How can you improve your relationships at work? How will you know when your relationships have improved? What difference will this make?

Focus
on strengths

The human person has intrinsic value. Father Biestek

What would your manager or colleagues say that you do well at work? What are the signs that you are doing good work? How will they keep track of these? What will reassure them?

Good managers help the team identify goals for improvement. They then allow the team members to get on with the job while acting as a source of support, appreciation and feedback.[9]

Some of the best managers I've worked with kept their focus on what's working well and expressed appreciation of the team's efforts. They particularly resisted pointing out what a person was doing wrong. Pointing out a problem to someone doesn't mean they'll be able to figure out what they should do differently.

If you're part of a team, instead of focusing on what is going wrong in your workplace, appreciate what your colleagues do well. If you are a manager, it's certainly important to help the team focus on what can be done better, but by drawing on strengths rather than highlighting weaknesses, a manager can inspire their team to achieve great things. And everyone will be happier in the process.

What are the strengths of your team in achieving your vision?

What good systems and practices do you have in place that keep you working well?

How is your workplace unique? What distinguishes it from others?

What is your organisation best at?

How do you draw on the specific skills and strengths of each person?

Create a
shared vision

Some look at things that are, and ask why? I dream things that never were, and ask why not? George Bernard Shaw

Goals give us direction and purpose. Developing a future vision for how your workplace can develop will help you to move towards that vision. Goals help promote optimism.

What does it take to make your vision a reality? Certainly it takes hard work and dedication, but it also takes the commitment of every member of a team to move closer to the goal. Think about a relay team. If only one member of the team is truly aiming to win that gold medal, what are the team's chances of success? What if just one runner is wishing he'd been a swimmer instead?

Set your goals with determination and with care. Your workplace goals should take into account the needs, abilities, skills and motivation of all the individuals you are asking to jump on board with your vision.

If you are a manager, draw on the experience and ideas of everyone in the workplace to form your vision. Sometimes, the most amazing ideas can come from the quietest team member. If you are a team member, this is a great chance to contribute to something that is bigger than you. Help to shape your workplace and the things your team spends its time and energy on.

How do you continue to innovate?

What sign would tell you that your team is growing stronger? What difference might it make?

What are the possibilities for improving your work?

How can you help others achieve their best?

What is your top priority?

CREATIVE CHALLENGE

Draft an article for a magazine about your workplace, projecting five years into the future. In the article, talk about the following: How is the organisation different? What do your colleagues say about you? What are your employees, clients or the public saying? Be concrete and include real quotes from people, actual numbers, and a clear description of a new product, service or process.

My commitment to engaging in work

My work situation is currently going well in these ways:

My goals for improving my working life are:

What has worked for me in the past is to:

Other sources of support and encouragement I can use are:

I can boost my confidence by:

My next step is to:

DOMAIN 7:
Building relationships

And then he gave a very long sigh and said, 'I wish Pooh were here. It's so much more friendly with two.' AA Milne in Winnie-the-Pooh

Take a moment to describe your three happiest moments that don't involve other people. Not easy, is it?

Good relationships are so essential to our wellbeing and happiness. Researchers have found that people who regularly see friends, relatives or neighbours are happier than those who don't.[10] They also found that people who have meaningful conversations are happier than those who make small talk.[29] Humans are social creatures — we need to love and be loved.

For many, getting married is a life event that results in much happiness.[9] Life satisfaction often peaks in the years before and just after marriage, and the happiness levels of most people remain higher than before marriage. People who are married have better financial security, and the cost of living reduces through shared expenses. Married couples also have better physical and mental health, use drugs and/or alcohol less and live longer. Because marriage involves connection, trust and companionship,[9] the happiness of spouses is often interdependent. If one partner is happy, the other is likely to be happy too. And the equality of happiness in a marriage is important for stability.

But married people are only happier if they perceive their relationship to be a good one.[9] People in poor-quality marriages are generally happier once separated. And single people are much happier than unhappily married people.

Whether you're married or single, the more engaged you are socially, the happier you're likely to be. You might attend social and cultural events, participate in sport or undertake volunteer activities.[9] It doesn't matter what you do, but the more you interact and care for the wellbeing of others, the stronger your own sense of wellbeing will become. While building positive relationships takes effort, engaging with others enhances our lives.

The Dalai Lama reminds us that we are all dependent on each other. Babies and children are dependent on their parents' and caregivers' love for their self-confidence and development. Children are more likely to stay connected to school when they feel that teachers care about them. We have more confidence in health professionals who are warm and caring in their approach. In everyday life, people who take an interest and delight in being with us become our friends.

Love and compassion are at the core of our happiness. Invest in your relationships and take time to connect with others. Greet people with a smile. Trust in others and see the best in them.

How do relationships play a role in creating and maintaining happiness in your life?

What can you do to enhance the quality of your relationships?

Make an artwork symbolising you and your relationships. Draw a circle, about the size of a 20-cent piece, representing yourself, in the centre of a large piece of paper. Now start creating even larger circles around you. Place the important people in your life in each of the circles. The closer you feel to someone, the closer they will be to you. Notice which people you place in which circle.

- **How would you describe each person in each circle in terms of the relationship between you and this person?**

- **How does each person in each circle influence your sense of happiness?**

- **What does your artwork tell you about what is important to you in close relationships?**

Develop **respectful** relationships

A warm smile is the universal language of kindness. William Arthur Ward

Respect is the foundation of a healthy relationship. In respectful relationships you are able to be yourself and have fun together. It's okay to have different opinions and interests and you don't have to spend all your spare time together. Respectful relationships allow you to say 'no' to things you don't want to do, to see friends and family when you want to, to express your opinions and beliefs, and to make your own decisions. If someone treats you with respect, you feel safe with them.

In respectful relationships, communication is open and truthful and decisions are made together. Love, like life, isn't without conflict. But if conflict occurs in a respectful relationship, try to resolve it so both people feel okay, even if your ideas differ. You can listen to each other, compromise, say sorry, and talk issues through. Both people should be able to admit being wrong and take responsibility for what they think, feel and do.

Couples show their love for each other by working to be more caring and considerate in the future. They take their partner's feelings into account and look for the best in them. And when they say, 'I love you,' it is backed up by loving behaviour.

Most importantly, in a respectful relationship, you feel good about yourself. If you find yourself in a relationship where your partner doesn't treat you with respect, for example, they put down your ideas or blame you for things not going their way — look for strengths in yourself and support from others to feel better about yourself. Then ask yourself if you would be happier and safer without the relationship. And this is important: What would you advise a good friend to do in your situation? Everyone deserves to be safe and respected.

How do your relationships contribute to feeling good about yourself?

What do you want from a relationship? What don't you want?

How do people show respect towards you? How do you show respect for others?

Keep **romance** alive

It is a fine seasoning for joy to think of those we love. Molière

Romantic relationships can provide some of our greatest joys and our steepest challenges. To love means to risk being hurt. But if we seek only to avoid rejection, we miss out on love. Many agree that love is worth the risk of being let down. To live a rich and full life, love as much as you can.

Take time to notice what keeps your relationship strong and what you value in a relationship. What do you appreciate and admire about your partner? What does your partner love and admire about you?

Consider how you show your love to each other: do you give compliments, do things for each other, or show your affection through gifts, touch or spending time together?[30] Are the ways you show affection the same as or different to your partner? How can you meet your partner's needs as well as your own?

Look for different ways to connect: send a text message, phone, email or leave little notes. Or be romantically old-fashioned and send letters — keep those you receive tied with a ribbon in a special place: they can become keepsakes. Buy flowers or a delicious treat for your partner for no reason other than to make them happy.

Spend time together doing things you enjoy. Hang out, cook a special meal, or go for a walk. Doing new and exciting things as often as possible can help the relationship feel fresh.

Intimate and sexual relationships are especially important to many people, and are a major part of the enjoyment of life. This is particularly so for people whose preferred way of expressing their affection is via touch.

Look for ways to keep romance alive. Telling your partner what you appreciate about them can never be underestimated. Keep your language positive — point out what you like about your partner. Look into each other's eyes. Hold hands. What keeps the spark alive in your relationship?

What builds happiness in your relationship? What do you enjoy doing together?

What first attracted you to each other?

What helps you to get through the tough times together?

What do you need to keep remembering is important to keep your relationship strong?

How can you enhance your intimacy?

Spend time with
people you enjoy

Let us be grateful to people who make us happy, they are the charming gardeners who make our souls blossom. Marcel Proust

Our connections with friends can bring us great happiness. Good friendships provide a sense of belonging, fun, support and inspiration. Sometimes, we connect because we share interests, values, likes and dislikes with our friends and sometimes friends are quite unalike, but have a synergy that is powerful. For some, friends are as important as (or even more important than) family.

Research into social networks shows happiness can spread from person to person, and niches of happiness form within social networks.[31] People surrounded by happy people are more likely to be happy themselves. So our happiness depends on the happiness of the people with whom we are connected.

Spending time with people you enjoy, catching up for coffee, having dinner with friends, playing cards and telling stories are some simple ways to grow joy in your life. Consider different ways to spend time together, perhaps by building in healthy routines such as a walk if you are trying to increase your activity levels. You could also volunteer together, or try a new sport or hobby. Sometimes, trying something new is less scary with a good friend.

If you're trying to make changes in your life, such as quitting smoking or losing weight, it's interesting to know that researchers have found that people who are overweight tend to be connected with others who are overweight,[32] and the same applies for smokers.[33] It makes sense that people close to you have similar lifestyles but it can make behaviour change even more challenging. Hanging out in new networks and making new friends might prove to be an important part of implementing lifestyle changes. Otherwise, try to enlist the support of your friends even if they are not ready to make the same changes themselves.

Friendships do need attention. Value your friends and see them as often as possible. Find small ways to let them know you appreciate them and how important they are. Is there someone you'd like to get back in touch with?

What do you value about your closest friends?

How do you show that you value them?

What difference has it made to your life to have these connections?

What do your friends value about you?

How do you support your friends and how do they support you?

INSPIRING IDEA

At the end of every year make amends to all those you are worried you may have wronged and let people know how much you appreciate them.

Celebrate your family and heritage

Keep love in your heart ... The consciousness of loving and being loved brings a warmth and a richness to life that nothing else can bring. Oscar Wilde

Family matters. Our family members are often the people we are most connected to throughout our life. They've known us the longest and, in many cases, know us the best. This sense of connectedness and belonging can be an important part of people's lives. For many, their greatest compliment is that their family are proud of them.

But it's not always the case. For some, happiness depends on keeping their family members at a safe distance. Practising compassion, forgiveness, tolerance and understanding is the key to living well. Many people whose birth families are not safe create their own families of friends: these are families of choice and relationships within them can be richly rewarding, supportive and nurturing.

Being part of a family can give people a stronger sense of where they've come from. Families have shared experiences and a shared history and heritage is retold as family stories. Families share rituals, habits and a common understanding of 'how things are done'. Families often also hold similar values and common skills and talents. Many people find they can pick up with family where they left off, even after long periods of separation.

But families are not always easy. You may not be able to choose your family, but you can choose what relationship you have with them. Ultimately, whether your family is a source of pleasure or pain is influenced by how you choose to relate with them. Where it's possible, make peace with your family and, if you can, find ways to celebrate both your family and heritage.

What do you value most about your family? In what way do you create your own values?

What things do you enjoy doing with your family?

What are some of your family's cherished stories and memories?

What important things about your cultural background shape who you are? In what ways do you celebrate and value your cultural origins?

INSPIRING IDEA

Begin a compliments box at home that each family member can contribute to. At the end of every week read out the compliments and give the slip of paper to that person to keep.

Show love and respect
to children in small ways as often as possible

Who, being loved, is poor? Oscar Wilde

Caring for kids can be demanding — perhaps that's why it is not highly rated in activities that contribute to happiness.[9] This is more so for parents of babies, toddlers and teenagers. Having children does not guarantee higher happiness levels; the extent to which you find happiness in raising your kids can be heavily influenced by the age and temperament of the children, the quality of the parenting couple, and the amount of time parents have available to enjoyably spend with their children.

Parents are incredibly strong influences on their children's wellbeing and happiness. Children develop confidence through the way they interact with others. Children who are praised feel confident and loved. Perhaps happiness, as a parent, comes from being proud of the positive contribution we make by giving our children a good start in life.

Involving children in daily tasks teaches them skills for life. It also gives you lovely opportunities to talk and spend time with your child while you do your daily activities. Parenting children involves both following their lead when you play together and knowing how to lead them when you are teaching them things.

Get your kids excited about cooking and food (a good thing for fussy eaters). Make it fun: draw on your pre-schooler's skills in stirring, stacking and building. Children can pluck herbs from their stems or tear basil leaves, exploring the different smells. They can wash fruit and vegetables (and learn about saving water), measure and mix ingredients (learning about numbers), arrange ingredients on pizza (patterns), or play word games eating alphabet soup (literacy). Children can help to mash vegetables (developing coordination) and make a snowman out of mashed potatoes, using other vegetables to make the arms, hat and face (fun!). Who knows … when they become teenagers they might even take turns to cook meals!

In the middle of the night, a screaming child who will not sleep may not seem like a source of happiness, but in just a moment that cute smile will make your heart melt and all will be right with the world.

What's the best thing about being a parent?

What aspects of your children make you feel like a great parent?

What are your hopes for your children?

What do you look forward to with your children?

Practise positive parenting

It is not a bad thing that children should occasionally,
and politely, put parents in their place. Colette

Self-confidence is one of the most valuable traits a parent can nurture in their child. Children develop confidence when adults treat them respectfully, and when they feel valued for who they are. When you encourage your child to express their opinions, contribute ideas and make choices about things that matter to them, you instil in your child a sense of their intrinsic value.[6] This builds their self-esteem and confidence. Self-esteem comes from how much they feel they matter to the people around them.

But encouraging your child to develop a healthy self-esteem also means providing boundaries and discipline to encourage positive growth. It's not about punishment: effective discipline involves working with your children, not against them, and is characterised by effective listening, clear and consistent communication, and modelling good behaviour. Children learn by example. They learn right from wrong by copying their parents. So, in all you do, think about what you want your children to learn: if you hit, then they may learn that it's okay to hit people when they do something they don't like.

Parents of teenagers say their young people can bring energy, excitement and fun into their life.[34] Young people can be great company and watching them grow into adults can bring a sense of pride. Few people would disagree that teens are also a challenge!

Parents of adolescents say their greatest challenge is dealing with feeling unappreciated. There are also times that you, as a parent, need to do what is right despite the resentment that comes back at you from your teen.

Positive parenting in the teenage years involves respecting your adolescent's need for space and keeping communication lines open. If your teen is open to it, have a regular catch-up time — perhaps over dinner on the weekend, or on the drive to sport or drama. It's important that your teen knows they can speak to you if they need to … but remember, they may choose not to.

Teenage years don't have to be characterised by conflict. Pick your battles and choose the important issues to be firm about. Most parents love their teenage child, but not the challenging behaviours. It helps to remember that it's all part of the developmental process — the hormones are just doing their job!

Most importantly, keep cool and take time out for yourself.

What do you do well as a parent?

When you think of being happy with your children what does that look like to you?

Describe the relationship you want with your children. How do you prefer to treat them and how do you prefer them to treat you?

What helps you most in your role of being a parent? Who supports you? Who could you call on for support?

Experience the
unconditional love
of a pet

*An animal's eyes have the power to speak
a great language.* Martin Buber

Owning a pet (or being owned by one!) can be deeply rewarding. Having a dog leap up and welcome you home or a cat who curls around your legs can make you feel needed and valued. Owning a pet can lead to opportunities for social interactions with other people and lessen loneliness and isolation. But for many people it is the ongoing unconditional love they receive from their pet that is the most fulfilling.

Our pets help us get through tough times. Having a companion and keeping up with daily routines can be important ways to promote wellbeing and reduce stress. The joy and sense of responsibility of caring for another being also brings fulfilment.

Many families have pets so children can experience the joy of growing up with an animal and learning to care for another being. Before you seek out a new pet, especially when choosing a pet for your children, think carefully about how the pet you're considering will fit with your family's lifestyle. Some dogs need long daily runs, while others are really indoor dogs. Some cats are particularly fond of stalking birds and wildlife, which you and your kids may find upsetting.

Pets are an important part of many families — and can be a lot easier than people to get along with! Pets don't answer back, at least not directly, but they might eat your shoes. If you adopt a pet from a pound or shelter you not only gain a new friend, you may save an animal from death row.

How would having a pet enrich your life?

What is the best thing about caring for a pet?

Practise
forgiveness

Forgiveness does not change the past,
but it does enlarge the future. Paul Boese

Sometimes increasing happiness involves making peace with the past. You might need to mend a rift in a relationship or repair past hurts by forgiving someone who has behaved badly towards you.

Forgiveness doesn't mean forgetting, but it does mean no longer being a victim. When you choose to forgive someone, you choose to not be held back by disappointment, hatred, hurt and resentment. It means choosing to let go of these things. You don't need to confront someone who has wronged you or even have direct contact with them. You can simply decide to forgive within yourself. Sometimes, writing a letter (which you can send or not send) can help you set the past free.

We can't change the past, nor can we make others take responsibility for things they refuse to. But we can change how we think about ourselves in relation to these events. Forgiveness releases us from the past and makes us a survivor, not a victim.

What would enable you to address your feelings about past events in order to live a happier future?

Are there people with whom you want to address a past event? What would enable you to do this? How might it make a difference?

How might making peace with the past liberate you? How might you become stronger as a result?

Treasure lost loves

*I love my past, I love my present. I am not ashamed
of what I have had, and I am not sad because
I no longer have it.* Colette

Friendships and relationships teach us about many things, including loss. Thinking about those who have died, or lost loves, can stir strong emotions, but it can also rekindle feelings of warmth and caring.

We can have ongoing close relationships with people who have died: they live on in our memories. What things and events remind you of them? When did you laugh together and enjoy each other's company? When memories feel alive, you're not living in the past: some moments never fade or die, so treasure your special memories together.

How do you honour those close to you who have died?

What did that person teach you that remains important in your life?

If you could, what would you say to them now?

How do you treasure their memory and cherish what they have contributed to your life?

My commitment to building my relationships

I am happy with my current family and other relationships in these ways:

My goals for improving my family and other relationships are:

What has worked for me in the past is to:

Other sources of support and encouragement I can use are:

I can boost my confidence by:

My next step is to:

DOMAIN 8:
Connecting with your community

Beginning today, treat everyone you meet as if they were going to be dead by midnight. Extend to them all the care, kindness and understanding you can muster, and do it with no thought of any reward. Your life will never be the same again. Og Mandino

For us to flourish as individuals, we must have freedom. Autonomy, or being able to act according to our values and desires uncontrolled by outside influences, is important for our wellbeing. But while happiness is linked to being free to shape your own future, we also need a sense of belonging and intimacy. Research has found that people who are connected to others have better supports and are happier.[35] And solitude, or not needing to relate to others, is associated with increased isolation and depression.

Many people do not get a fair go in life. Every night, too many people experience some form of homelessness. People are victims of robbery, physical or sexual assault, or threats of violence. Some groups of people have poorer health, lower life expectancy and are more likely to be victims of crime compared to others, even when they put in a great deal of effort individually.

Inequalities in wealth have been increasing. Worldwide, it is estimated that the richest 2 per cent of the population own more than half of total global wealth.[36] Equity promotes a sense of fairness and more trust — and overall people are happier. The reverse is also true: happiness declines when inequalities increase.[9]

Many people have regular contact with family and friends and feel they can rely on others in times of need. Most also feel that they can ask people not living with them for small favours or help in a time of crisis, and thankfully, people contribute to the wider community through volunteering or by donating to charities.

Be a part of your community. Take time to connect with others. Volunteer and support others. Be inspired and inspire others, encouraging them to join in. Participate in making our world a better place so people can connect, feel safe and be valued. Respect all living creatures and celebrate our common humanity as well as our individual differences.

In what ways do you notice society's values are changing? What is your response to this?

What are the values you subscribe to?

How do you show respect for all people, including yourself?

CREATIVE CHALLENGE

Make a picture reflecting how you would like the world to be. Highlight the signs that some of these things are already happening as part of the world you live in.

- **What contribution can you start making that will help make the world a better place?**

Take time to **connect**

A person with 'Ubuntu' is open and available to others, affirming of others, does not feel threatened that others are able and good, for he or she has a proper self-assurance that comes from knowing that he or she belongs in a greater whole. Archbishop Desmond Tutu

Feeling connected to people in your local community creates a sense of belonging, which enhances happiness and wellbeing.

One way to connect with your local community is to simply spend time on the street and in communal areas such as parks. Walk your dog in the local area, take your kids to the park, or go for a picnic in a popular spot. Perhaps set yourself the challenge of talking to one person you don't know each day.

Local councils and associations are a good source of information about community events, activities and resources. Find out what's happening and take part in street parties, festivals and community arts events. Create a chess competition at a picnic table near the local shopping centre. Visit a local library, gallery or museum. Go for a swim at your local beach or swimming pool.

Another way to meet locals is to belong to a community organisation, club or interest group. Attend sporting events or participate in sports. Get involved in local classes and community colleges. Do some gardening and meet new people at your local community garden.

Get to know your neighbours: chat to shopkeepers or talk with people waiting for the bus. Invite your neighbours to bring a plate and meet at your place, or if your place is too small, perhaps meet at your local park for a picnic.

Would it surprise you to learn that research has found that people who watch more television are less happy? When television was first introduced in Canada, one town received it significantly later than the others. Researchers were able to demonstrate that, when TV was introduced, social life reduced and aggression increased.[9]

One night there was a blackout in our street. Everyone came out of their apartments with candles, met in the street and spoke to neighbours they did not know. Later we played the guitar and told stories by candlelight. People connecting, in a way they did not usually do, made it a fun evening. Adversity can bring opportunity.

Be a change-maker. Look for ways to make your community better, not just complain about it. Attend community events and forums. Listen to community radio and become a subscriber. Read local papers and talk with people — know what's happing in your community. Consider sending a photo, story or letter to a local newsletter, magazine or newspaper. Join the local branch of a political party and be politically active.

Celebrate our diverse community by getting involved with cultural events, exploring different foods, music, stories and customs. Take time to connect and enjoy being with people in your community.

What brings your local community together?

How do you connect with your local community?

Which locally based activities do you currently do? Which ones would you like to do?

What do you know about your neighbours?

In what way do you connect with people from other cultures?

Help others

The place to be happy is here. The time to be happy is now.
The way to be happy is to make others so. Robert Ingersoll

Doing something for someone else is good for both you and them. Research has found that people who performed three acts of kindness per day became happier.[24] And happier people are also more likely to help others.[12] The more we help, the more likely we are to keep helping — because it feels good.

One great way to give while connecting with others in your local community is to volunteer or do some *pro bono* (unpaid) work. People who volunteer often say they get more out of it than they put in. Research says volunteering can be a great way to create happiness because it generates a stronger sense of life satisfaction, greater self-esteem, a sense of control over life, better physical health, and less depression.[37]

If you are time poor, you can still give. Consider donating to a charity. And, if you have more time on your hands, think about using some of it to volunteer. Support your local school or sporting group or become an overseas volunteer. Think about being on the committee or board of a local organisation, helping the elderly with jobs such as gardening, delivering food to people in need or helping with reading at a primary school. You can find volunteer opportunities in local newspapers, community noticeboards, websites or volunteering centres.

It can be of great value to notice and acknowledge local acts of kindness: positive things people do for others. A character who lives in my suburb often calls out to passers-by, 'You're beautiful,' bringing a smile to their faces. I am always struck by his cheery disposition, despite physical and intellectual difficulties. He frequently walks neighbours' dogs and cleans a nearby beach. When we call out, 'You're doing a great job,' he replies, 'Thank you. I appreciate being appreciated.'

By sharing and caring for each other we help to create a more tolerant and inclusive society. And for the people we help, we show them they are loved, not forgotten, and that someone cares. Helping others to be happy also makes us happy.

Who are the people that you support? How does supporting them add value to your life?

What have you discovered about your qualities, abilities, skills, knowledge and attitudes from supporting others?

What would the people you have supported say about the kind of person you are and what you can be proud of?

INSPIRING IDEA

Practise simple, deliberate and thoughtful acts of kindness throughout your day.

Value traditional cultures

If you listen to your heart, you can create something really big. Jessica Mauboy

So many countries are in the unique position of being able to draw on the rich and long history of their indigenous people, recognising and respecting their special place, culture and contribution as the first inhabitants. The oldest civilisations have a strong connection to land and country. Remote communities are often part of a nation's heritage, preserving traditional languages and ways of life.

However, many indigenous communities are home to some of the poorest people in a country. Indigenous people tend to have lower life expectancies than non-indigenous people, and often have higher rates of illness and disease. Some communities still don't have access to clean water or secure housing.

If we are to truly value indigenous culture, we need to start valuing indigenous happiness. What can you do to start bettering the lives of indigenous people? How can you contribute?

Around the globe there is a growing appreciation of the value of understanding the history of the land; the rich tradition of indigenous culture; and the importance of connecting with indigenous people. One way to better appreciate traditional culture is to attend cultural events. Talk with indigenous people about their history, their lives and the challenges they face. You will deepen your insight and understanding of their perspectives, challenges and strength.

What do you appreciate about indigenous culture?

How can you learn more about indigenous culture?

What increases your confidence that there can be better connections between non-indigenous and indigenous people?

How can you participate in events that celebrate indigenous culture?

How can you become involved in promoting the rights of indigenous peoples?

Get active to change the big picture

You must be the change you wish to see in the world. Mahatma Gandhi

There's so much room for improvement in our society. There's no point in a person wanting to eat better if they can't afford fruit and vegetables. It's hard to choose an environmentally sound washing machine if all the cheap ones have poor energy ratings. It's a challenge to cut down your driving if there is no public transport in your suburb. How do we spend more time with family if affording a house means a two-hour commute? How do we get fit and get involved in the community if it's not safe to walk or cycle around the local streets?

The list can feel overwhelming. But people can make a difference. There are many examples of community initiatives where people have made great improvements in their local areas: cycleways, footpaths and good lighting make physical exercise easier; food co-ops and farmers' markets increase the availability of fresh and affordable food; community celebrations get people together and help to celebrate our diverse cultures and increase social connections. Next time you vote, think about whether you are voting in the community's best interest or your own.

On the global scale, think about how you engage with social issues and take action for social change. You can join groups who are trying to make changes or make your own connections using social networking websites. The internet can be a useful resource to connect with others who want to get active to change the world for the better. Join an online community to campaign for peaceful solutions to the world's problems. Join a group that campaigns for human rights or an environmental lobby group. Stand up for what you believe in.

How can you make a difference in making our world a better place?

What can you do to get involved with tackling social issues?

How do you connect with others to share your vision?

What possibilities do you get excited about?

What collaboration and partnerships make change seem more achievable?

Help create a safe and caring community

The ultimate measure of a man is not where he stands in moments of comfort and convenience, but where he stands at times of challenge and controversy. Martin Luther King Jr.

When society is working well, there are high levels of trust. Social connection and trust are important to life satisfaction.[12] Although we might find it easier to connect with people who are similar to us, we also want to trust people we perceive as being different to us. Trust between people goes beyond social groupings, such as whether people are young or old, male or female, gay or straight, or from different cultural backgrounds.[9] In order to feel trust, people need to feel safe. If we feel safe, we have confidence and freedom. And, of course, happiness follows.

Unfortunately, violence is all too common in our communities. Every day, men and women experience violence in our homes, our workplaces and our communities. This violence includes physical and sexual assault, domestic violence and threatening behaviour.

Many victims of violence know their attacker. Most women who have been sexually assaulted knew the perpetrator. Most perpetrators of child sexual assault are known to the family. And domestic or family violence, by its nature, occurs between people who are in a relationship.

For a range of reasons, many victims of violence do not report the incident to police or seek professional help. They may not even perceive the violence as a crime. We know that victims of crime frequently experience mental-health problems, including depression, anxiety disorders, drug or alcohol abuse, and suicide.

Some communities have worked together to improve the safety of their locality as a whole, and to send the message that violence will not be tolerated. These movements draw both women and men who feel passionately that we must change community attitudes to improve the safety of all members of society. Some groups work with police to increase safety through changes such as improved lighting, fixing public telephones and improving public transport. Creating safer local environments helps people in the community to feel safer.

Another way to stand up to violence is to get to know the people in your community. If you know of situations of violence, whatever it might be, think about how you can reach out in support. Often, victims feel very isolated and powerless to change their situation, but the help of a friend or neighbour can make a huge difference. Don't be afraid to contact the police, even if you do it anonymously.

How can you help make your community safer?

How do you make a stand against violence and discrimination in your community?

Create enriching
environments for all

It takes a whole village to raise a child. Africa proverb

The Universal Declaration of Human Rights says: 'All human beings are born free and equal in dignity and rights.'[38] An inclusive society where everyone can participate as fully and equally as possible is important.

The concept of 'social inclusion' is concerned with how well people can participate in daily life. We have a responsibility to help shape a world in which all are freely able to participate, particularly the more vulnerable members of our community, such as children, young people, the elderly and those with disabilities.

Children thrive in enriching environments. A child-friendly community is one in which children are valued, supported, respected, provided for and actively included. Children who can play safely and who feel valued have the best opportunities to develop and grow. Children who feel that justice is upheld at school feel safe and more positive about being at school.[39] Support from teachers significantly increases a student's happiness.[40]

Young people with a long-term illness or disability say they achieve a sense of wellbeing when they feel supported, have opportunities for personal growth, and can live a normal life integrated in society.[41]

There are many ways we can change things for people with disabilities: providing opportunities for participation in sports and leisure activities, education and work, regardless of physical or intellectual ability or disability. In a study of patients with locked-in syndrome, a condition where despite being conscious their only movement is via eye movements, about one-third were unhappy. Their unhappiness was linked to dissatisfaction with mobility in the community and access to recreational activities.[42]

An elder-friendly community is one in which the strengths and capabilities of older people are valued and encouraged. Our population is getting older, and older people are increasingly involved in the care of grandchildren, participating in parenting and teaching values in children and young people. Many grandparents have more time to play with children, take them to interesting places and teach them about the world. Elders have valuable knowledge that can be handed down to younger generations, such as family history, family recipes, stories and jokes.

Many older people volunteer or work part-time as well as participate in community activities. In turn, many elderly people benefit from the support of a friendly neighbour or family member driving them to the shops or calling to say hello. With a little support, elderly people can often stay living at home longer.

By understanding the needs of all the groups in our community we can help everyone fully participate in living a rich and fulfilling life.

How do you involve children and young people in planning for the future?

How do you draw on the experience and wisdom elderly people offer your community?

What can you do to enable others to participate more fully?

My commitment to connecting with my community

I currently connect with the broader community by:

My goals for improving connection with the broader community are:

What has worked for me in the past is to:

Other sources of support and encouragement I can use are:

I can boost my confidence by:

My next step is to:

DOMAIN 9:
Caring for the environment

We know it well that none of us acting alone can achieve success. We must therefore act together as a united people. Nelson Mandela

Unless we make some significant changes to the way we live, eat, travel and do business, the prospects for our environment appear bleak. In particular, our current pattern of economic growth is simply not environmentally sustainable. Sitting with this reality can trigger a strong sense of vulnerability, and that vulnerability seems to prompt a lot of people to stick their fingers in their ears, close their eyes and hope it will all just go away.

On the upside, we have a wealth of information now about real changes we can make. If we can ease our anxiety long enough to act on our awareness, we can regain a sense of control by making changes in our daily lives.

Importantly, people are becoming disillusioned with the idea that economic advancement is the key to a better world and are looking for a new set of values. We can make real and sustainable changes when we are more thoughtful of the planet's needs and the needs of future generations.

The quest for happiness is intimately linked to the quest for sustainable development. The United Nations' *World Happiness Report*[25] says:

> If we continue mindlessly along the current economic trajectory, we risk undermining the Earth's life support systems — food supplies, clean water, and stable climate — necessary for human health and even survival in some places. On the other hand, if we act wisely, we can protect the Earth while raising quality of life broadly around the world. We can do this by adopting lifestyles and technologies that improve happiness (or life satisfaction) while reducing human damage to the environment.

Changing our lifestyle to become more environmentally friendly is not just about caring for the future; it may help us to live healthier and happier lives right now. By refusing to deny what we know to be true, we live more authentically in ourselves and our communities. By reducing the pollutants we contribute to the world, we make choices that are also healthier for us as individuals.

Many people go beyond changing their own behaviour to getting active within their communities. They talk to friends and workmates, attend community events, or volunteer to support an environmental action group to lobby for change. Joining a group can be a great way to connect with others. There are lots of environmental groups and climate-change organisations, as well as groups active in cleaning up local parks and rivers. Investigate the groups in your area and how you can become part of them.

What is more important to you: sustainable development or material progress?

How have your values shaped your views about sustainability?

How can you become more involved with tackling environmental issues?

Apart from being better for the environment, what other benefits would come from reducing consumption and recycling more?

How can you get involved to promote awareness of environmental issues to the broader community?

CREATIVE CHALLENGE

Think of a seemingly unsolvable problem like climate change. What would be an outrageous solution to the problem? Write, draw or paint the solution.

- What is your wildest idea for solving the problem?
- Is there one part of this idea that might be modified to make it more do-able?
- Does it suggest a direction that can be followed?
- Are there any other ideas that are possibilities?

Cultivate your appreciation of nature

Look deep into nature, and then you will understand everything better. Albert Einstein

Childhood experiences of nature — the family camping trip, holidays at the beach, playing in the park — can sow the seeds of environmental passion. It's so important that our children and teens are exposed as often as possible to natural experiences.

Adults, too, need time with nature to appreciate its inherent beauty, otherwise caring for the environment becomes an academic self-preservation exercise. Nature's smallest gifts, like birdsong in the morning, can bring great joy to the day.

As an urban or suburban sanity-saving measure, if you can't get into nature at its best, get out to a local park as often as you can. Devote space to a garden that contains at least a corner somewhere with a wild, dense, diverse green canopy where you can sit and think. Try an outdoor room, such as a deck or seating area surrounded by wildly luscious plants. Or you may like to get involved with your local community garden.

A great volunteering opportunity and way to cultivate your appreciation for nature is to join a team to restore walking tracks though bush areas or along beaches. Other ways to connect with nature include bush or coastal walks, walking in the rain, swimming in the ocean, and visiting an aquarium or zoo.

In what ways do you get in touch with nature?

How can you simplify your life and enjoy natural spaces more?

How do you teach children about being environmentally friendly?

Walk and cycle
whenever you can

Beware the barrenness of a busy life. Socrates

O besity rates are increasing, oil prices are skyrocketing — making holes in our weekly finances — and time wasted in traffic is increasing by the day. And these are just some of the personal impacts of daily travel. But we also know that carbon and pollutant emissions from motorised transport are a huge problem for the environment. Travel, by any means other than your feet or bicycle, leaves both a personal and an environmental footprint.

When we walk or cycle we experience the pleasures (and challenges) that being outdoors offers. When I rediscovered cycling as an adult, I loved the joy of feeling like a kid riding a bicycle again. There's something just plain fun about riding a bike. And when most of us struggle to fit in exercise as part of our daily routine, commuting by walking or riding a bicycle makes good sense — even if it takes a little longer than our usual method.

If you drive to work, are there alternatives? As the costs of running a car rise, and as bus and train facilities improve, public transport becomes a more relaxing option. Public transport can be a great time to meditate, learn something new, listen to music or read a book. Bring a camera with you and take snaps of the things that catch your eye. If you really do need to drive to work, think about forming a car pool.

This way you can avoid being yet another single-occupant car in the overcrowded lanes of other single-occupant cars.

On weekends or when you're out, coordinate car trips so everything possible is done at once rather than making multiple trips. Try to buy in bulk.

When you fly, think about carbon offsetting. A small fee helps mitigate greenhouse gas emissions by purchasing carbon offsets. When flying is unavoidable, at least you're reducing your overall emissions.

What are some ways you can improve your lifestyle and be more environmentally friendly at the same time?

Are there more opportunities for you to leave the car at home?

When can you walk or cycle more often?

INSPIRING IDEA

Negotiate with your boss to work from home to save on travel to work while reducing your carbon footprint. Otherwise, do some of your work while travelling on public transport.

Reduce, reuse, recycle

To enjoy life, we must touch much of it lightly. Voltaire

Many people are becoming increasingly passionate about sustainable living as the key to the future. We know that we can't solve environmental problems by simply buying and using 'green products'. Green consumption and recycling helps, but we desperately need to reduce our consumption.

Stay focused on what you can do to use less. Set yourself specific goals that are achievable in your everyday life. Talk with the people you live with and keep encouraging yourself and each other. Be mindful that you will not only be helping the planet, but you may be improving your health and saving money as well.

Save water by choosing appliances with a high water-efficiency rating, and use your washing machine and dishwasher only when you have a full load. You can also reduce water wastage by washing fruit and vegetables or rinsing dishes in a plugged sink or bowl instead of under running water. Turn off the tap while cleaning your teeth and (here's a challenging one) limit your time in the shower to three minutes. Cut hot-water usage by installing a water-efficient showerhead and use cold water for washing clothes. If you can, install a solar hot-water system. Using the sun to dry clothes is the best way to reduce your electricity bill naturally.

In the garden, add mulch to garden beds and potted plants to reduce the amount of water they need. Reduce evaporation by covering your pool, use a trigger nozzle on your hose and water the garden during the cooler parts of the day. Wash vehicles, outdoor furniture and the family pet on the grass. Install a rainwater tank or other collection-and-diversion devices and choose native plants and grasses that require less water than exotic species. Use a broom to clear and clean hard surfaces.

Keep your home comfortable with external shading such as eaves, awnings, shutters or trees to reduce heat. Install good insulation that will keep your home warmer in winter. Manage home heating and cooling by setting thermostats appropriately. Put on more or take off clothing before turning on the air conditioning. In fact, do you really need an air conditioner?

Switch off lights, appliances and equipment when they're not needed. Think seriously about whether you need a second fridge — they're a huge drain on electricity. Install energy-efficient lighting such as compact fluorescent bulbs. Choose appliances with a high energy star rating and use the energy-saving settings on your appliances. One of the easiest things you can do is to switch your energy to a green power source — contact your energy provider.

Consider your lifestyle and what you can do to care for the environment. There may be many things you are doing already, some that you can make a good effort to begin doing from now on, and others that may be just not possible right now but could be reconsidered again in the future.

How do you care for the environment? What do you do well?

What can you improve? What are some easy ways you can make a difference?

Reduce waste

Don't use a whole lot when a little will do. Proverb

R ecently I heard waste referred to as a form of greed. Although it seemed a strong statement, when I thought about it more it made sense because waste denies resources to people in need who can make good use of them. And waste depletes energy and resources, which we don't have to spare.

Every day, restaurants waste large amounts of good uneaten food, supermarkets discard large quantities of close-to-date products, and growers discard perfectly edible produce that is not the right size or shape for the market. Unused food goes straight into the bin from the refrigerator in many households. Fishermen throw unfashionable fish back into the sea — dead — even though they are equally as good as popular market fish.

But there are also good examples of programs and individuals challenging our wasteful practices. Charities collect unused food from restaurants and deliver it to services that support the homeless. Artists collect 'found objects' and use them to create art. The increasing popularity of recycled fashion, clothing swap parties and second-hand websites are evidence that we're increasingly looking to make the most of things that others no longer need. Perhaps we could see a return to past practices where gleaners combed crops, foraging for produce left behind so it would not be wasted.

There are many ways to release yourself from the stuff you don't use — from advertising it on a website, to offering it to a neighbour or friend, or leaving it on the nature strip with a note attached. Garage sales are a fabulous way to de-clutter, meet neighbours, save landfill and make money.

Shop smartly to avoid waste. Look for products that aren't over-packaged and choose products that have recycled content. Be mindful of purchasing stuff you don't really need. If I see something I like, but am not sure I really need, my tactic is to simply keep it in mind — and come back later if I decide to buy it. While I might have missed out on a few things I've gone back for, I've also saved myself from many unnecessary impulse purchases.

Shop critically, by asking questions: 'Do I really need this?', 'Can I afford this?' and 'Will buying this thing take me in the direction I want to go?' Answering these three questions will help you make good decisions. Shop with a list so that you're not tempted to buy things you don't need.

I have a friend who made a New Year's resolution to wear all of the clothes in her wardrobe and to buy less. Everyone, including the environment, benefits from wardrobe experiments!

How can you actively reduce waste?

How can you be the change that the world needs?

Detox your home

Act as if what you do makes a difference. It does. William James

Advertising companies get paid huge sums to convince us that every inch of our home should be bleached, sanitised, disinfected and kept free of germs — for our own safety. What they don't say is that hospitals stopped using bleach years ago because it is toxic to inhale. Many people are allergic to chemical products and fragrances too. Using fewer chemicals is not only cheaper and better for the environment, it is healthier too.

Green cleaning products include soap and water, bicarbonate of soda, white vinegar, and environmentally friendly products readily available at supermarkets. Orange oil is a great cleaner, but make sure that the one you choose isn't just orange-scented chemicals in disguise. Older family members and people in your neighbourhood might have recipes for very effective, natural cleaners.

For health reasons, many people find they are better off without carpet and enjoy natural floorboards much more. Use beeswax polish to protect and rejuvenate wood and furniture. Use water-based and natural plant-based paints.

Try not to rely on chemicals to control pests. Prevent access to your home with flyscreens and make sure you fix leaks and seal cracks and crevices. Don't leave food around to act as an attractant. And, as a last line of defence, choose low-toxic ways to repel pests. Plant-based insect repellents include eucalyptus, tea tree, lemongrass and citronella oil.

Composting and companion planting can reduce the need for pesticides and herbicides in the garden. And by buying organic produce, you can consume fewer chemicals and support local businesses too.

Like so many green choices, the alternatives to our usual way of life are healthier, cheaper, and better for the environment too. They just make us feel better — and therefore happier.

How can you change the way you clean to promote better health and protect the environment?

In what ways would you be able to make use of the benefits of organic gardening?

Make environmentally friendly changes at work

We shall require a substantially new manner of thinking if mankind is to survive. Albert Einstein

Are you environmentally conscious at home, but less so at work? Many of the ideas we've already explored are equally important and effective in your workplace.

Technology is making it easier to cut down on paper use. Think before you print, and when you do, make it double-sided. Buy recycled products and reuse whenever possible. You can get another use (or three) out of envelopes and manila folders by using adhesive labels. Use unwanted printed paper for children's drawings.

Use video conferencing or Skype instead of driving or flying to meetings and buy carbon credits to offset your flights. Laptops use less energy than regular computers. Change to energy-efficient light globes and switch to green power. Turn off the air conditioning whenever possible and turn off lights and computers at night.

We formed a group to support environmental changes in our workplace and it's not only been effective (with significant savings in cost and waste), it's also been great fun. Communal litter-less lunches, where we share a dish made from locally produced food that is then stored in reusable containers, helps keep enthusiasm high. Regular quizzes increase people's knowledge and help us measure improvements. Being green not only brings people together and helps us feel better about our workplaces, we can promote our efforts proudly and encourage others to try the same things. How can you reduce, reuse and recycle at your workplace?

What can you do to make your workplace more environmentally friendly?

My commitment to caring for the environment

Things I am currently doing well when it comes to living sustainably are:

My goals for improving how I care for the environment are:

What has worked for me in the past is to:

Other sources of support and encouragement I can use are:

I can boost my confidence by:

My next step is to:

DOMAIN 10:
Having fun

Because of your smile, you make life more beautiful. Thich Nhat Hanh

Sometimes having fun is about relaxing and switching off. Making time for just having fun is one of the easiest steps you can take to happiness. Leisure time can also be about doing something that engages you so deeply that time passes and you don't even notice it. Sometimes your leisure activities coincide with the idea of a personal challenge, or perhaps something that might be closer to a calling or a vocation.

Psychologist Martin Seligman describes three kinds of happiness: The Pleasant Life, the Good Life and the Meaningful Life.[43] The Pleasant Life involves positive emotions and things we like doing. The Good Life involves using your strengths and drawing on resources to make a difference to improve a situation. The Meaningful Life is about using your strengths and virtues in the service of something else to bring a wider meaning to your life. Living a meaningful life brings about the highest level of sustained happiness.

Consider your balance between passive and active leisure. If watching TV is your main means of relaxation, perhaps think about the amount of time you spend doing it and what other kinds of things might also bring enjoyment. Being engaged in active, creative hobbies can create extra happiness in your day. Think about what kinds of leisure activities also enrich your relationships and are positive for the people you live with.

Ideally, your relaxation and leisure time consists of a mix of different types of activities: things you enjoy just for fun, a pastime that uses your skills or something that challenges you even more. Having fun helps us feel that life is worth living.

What leisure activities do you enjoy most?

What do you find to be restorative and relaxing?

How can you make the most of your leisure time?

What kinds of leisure activities do you find enriching for you and the people you live with?

CREATIVE CHALLENGE

Make an artwork describing yourself doing something you enjoy. What makes it special for you and others?

Perhaps do this activity with your children using play dough or plasticine. Make sculptures representing the things that you enjoy doing or make people shapes and act out scenes of fun times together. Talk with your children and plan other fun things to do together.

Read a book

Do not read, as children do, to amuse yourself, or like the ambitious, for the purpose of instruction. No, read in order to live. Gustave Flaubert

For many, simply curling up on the couch on a Sunday reading a book and having nowhere else to go is blissful. For others, this seems like the height of laziness. But reading is so much more than taking time out to 'do nothing'. Reading can be incredibly rewarding because it can introduce you to new ideas and expand your awareness of the world.

Broaden your reading horizons. Read book reviews online or in weekend newspapers and magazines. Ask friends, the local librarian or your bookseller for recommendations. Consider starting a book club or reading group. Try reading something completely new then strike up a conversation about it — share your ideas and passions. If you are pressed for time, why not consider shorter pieces, such as poetry or short stories.

Or you might like to put pen to paper and write something yourself — a poem, short (or long) story, memoir or even a play. Being cultured means to respond to culture, and the best way to do this is to create your own.

What do you enjoy reading?

When are the best times for you to read?

What is your favourite book and why?

Listen to music

Music is the mediator between the spiritual and the sensual life. Ludwig van Beethoven

Hands up if you love music and couldn't live without it! Playing a musical instrument, dancing, singing, listening — there are so many ways in which music brings happiness.

It is not surprising that neuroscientists have found that music activates the pleasure zones of the brain in a similar way to other pleasures such as sexual orgasm, drugs and chocolate.[44] One of my favourite ways to enjoy music is to put on some rhythms that make me feel good and dance around the lounge room. This can be a great activity for kids too.

It can be a great pleasure to listen to music alone, especially when delving into your collection brings back moods and memories. Music is also a great way to connect with others if you join a band or choir. Learning to dance, playing an instrument or seeing a live band can be great ways to meet people.

Beethoven continued to create masterpieces even after he went deaf, composing some of his best works at this time. His passion was not only for music, but also for life. The sheer volume of his work is incredible, given the struggles in his life — health issues (including pain, deafness and mental-health problems) and being a carer for his two younger brothers.

Music can bring meaning to your life or even a whole new self-identity. Some people's experience of music has been profound, to the extent that it has changed their lives: think of 1960s folk, 1970s disco or punk, '80s pop, '90s drum and bass.

Whether you are into classical, folk, rock, hip-hop, jazz, pop, world music or a mixture of styles, try broadening your musical horizons by discovering new songs on the radio or online.

What kinds of music do you enjoy?

What opportunities are there for you to listen to music?

Do you have a song that inspires you?

Get cultural

When making your choice in life, do not neglect to live. Samuel Johnson

Fascinating, rewarding and absorbing cultural activities such as film, art and theatre enrich our lives. The arts are also a way we can share our stories and explore the meaning of our experiences.

Norwegian research has found that people who participated in cultural activities were more satisfied with their lives, although men preferred to be spectators, whereas woman liked to participate actively.[45]

Many people enjoy films and talking about them. From hosting a *Star Wars* movie day to watching *Gone With the Wind* with your grandmother, watching films is a fun thing to do. Going to the cinema is a great option for a date. Consider starting a movie club — enjoy and explore cinema with a group of friends. Avid moviegoers love to spend time analysing a movie, looking at the camera angles, the script, the lighting, the direction and the acting. They pore over every detail of the film to find out what it's saying to them or if it is saying anything at all.

But you don't need to interpret a film to enjoy it. Watching films can simply be a great way to see or experience something you wouldn't in daily life. Foreign films offer a peek into other cultures. Try exploring different periods and genres: think early Hollywood, spaghetti Westerns, French comedies, or Chinese sword-and-sandal epics — so much variety, so little time.

Like cinema, viewing art can also make us feel more engaged and alive. Taking hold of our imagination, art helps us see things in a different way. All of a sudden, we feel present in the moment, and this awareness helps us to live mindfully. Visiting an art gallery is often a wonderful experience; art openings can be especially fun. And, of course, there is a wealth of material online. Many people enjoy collecting original artworks (local and emerging artists can be more affordable). A striking or unique print, painting or sculpture can define a whole room and uplift your spirit each time you see it.

There is something very immediate about theatre that can be quite confronting, but also uniquely engaging. Being right there with the actors, sensing their emotions and watching the story unfold while also being aware of you as the viewer in the audience, can be an experience like no other.

What role does the arts play in your life?

What opportunities do you have for going to cultural events?

How can you make the most of these opportunities?

Create

Creativity takes courage. Henri Matisse

Creative activities are often some of our more inspired moments. While there are many opportunities to be creative in our lives, our leisure time is where we have the greatest opportunity to express ourselves. Creative activities can help you develop perspective and insight and discover more about yourself.

Have you ever been so absorbed or engrossed in an activity that you lost track of time? This is known as 'being in the zone' or 'flow'. Your full attention is focused on the activity and there is an experience of intensity that is also effortless. Problems are forgotten, yet you also become more self-aware. You are not distracted by other thoughts and you want it to go on forever. Researchers have found that flow states that come from being engaged in self-directed, goal-oriented, meaningful activity can produce a high level of happiness.[46]

Why not get out your paintbrushes and create some art — or forget the brushes and finger paint instead. There are so many different kinds of art forms to try: sculpture, photography, ceramics, printmaking, life drawing, making installations and digital media. Consider getting a painting group together and make an occasion of it.

Crafts offer another great opportunity to explore your creativity. Many involve skills handed down through generations. Check out your local community college or craft shop for ideas. You might like to get handy with a set of tools by learning woodwork or restoring an old piece of furniture, making mosaics or leadlight windows. Or it could be home crafts that warm your soul such as knitting, hand spinning, weaving or patchwork quilting. You can also paint T-shirts for your own unique look. Try silk screen-printing or jewellery making.

What would you love to try if you had the chance? Take the chance now.

How do you express creativity in your life?

Which creative activities inspire you? What gets you excited, enthusiastic and in a state of wonder?

What activities do you get lost in and lose track of time doing?

In what ways are these activities satisfying?

Play a sport

Happiness seems made to be shared. Pierre Corneille

Sport can be one of the great pleasures in life, both to play and to watch. Investing time and energy in a sport is an excellent release from the rest of life. Being in the zone, or experiencing flow, is also part of the sport experience — the feeling that nothing else matters. The diversity and range of sports available means almost everyone can find something interesting to play or watch.

There are few better feelings than the thrill of competition. Whether it is as part of a team or climbing a mountain, the natural high you get from sport makes you feel great. The benefits from exercising regularly are well known. Even a short early-morning run will boost your energy, while the simple pleasure of teeing off as the sun rises with dew on the ground can last the whole day.

Watching kids give their best to a game, while having fun doing it, can be a joy for you and an excellent learning experience for children too. Sport promotes friendship, teaches children about teamwork, and gives them the coping skills to meet challenges.

Watching your favourite team go round after winning a game is like seeing your favourite movie for the first time every weekend. Riding every bump, cheering, yelling, investing your emotional energy in the ecstasy of victory and the agony of defeat is all part of the package.

When you follow a team, you are part of a family. Some even describe their sport as a religion, or a code of ethics. The sense of belonging is a wonderful thing to see as strangers exchange stories and high fives as the team scores, or a packed stadium comes together as one to sing the national anthem before a big game. And if you are a long-term supporter, to see your team finally triumph after years in the wilderness is an amazing feeling.

What sports do you enjoy playing?

Which sports bring excitement to your life?

Do one thing you've **always wanted** to do

If we did all the things we are capable of, we would literally astound ourselves. Thomas A. Edison

Do you have a personal challenge, a skill you want to develop or a long-held dream? It may be that you long for an adventure: to travel overseas, take a road trip, climb a mountain, go boating, skiing, hiking or camping. Perhaps your challenge is to create an artwork, write a book, make a film, hold an exhibition or form a band.

Apart from gaining a sense of fulfilment and achievement from day-to-day activities and pursuits, many people find themselves wanting to take on a personal challenge. This may be learning a new skill, a creative project or achieving a personal goal. This could be something newly discovered or an old dream, even completing an unfinished project.

Have you ever travelled to a country where they don't speak English and felt like a goose because other travellers, usually from Europe, speak six languages? Learning a language can be a lot of fun, and can expand the mind. Why not study the language of a country you want to holiday in? It will help build your excitement as you learn more about the language, people and culture. And if you keep at it, new worlds will open up.

Your dream might be closer to home. You might want to create a collection, a wonderful garden or restore a piece of furniture. It might involve learning a dance or a musical instrument, to play chess or even to make home brew. Attending a class at your local community college could be a great first step towards becoming a better cook, learning to sew or knit, taking better photographs, mastering public speaking or becoming knowledgeable about wines.

Some challenges might lead you to train towards achieving a goal such as participating in a long distance race. It's never too late to do that one thing you've always wanted to do.

> **What do you dream of doing? What personal challenge would you like to achieve?**
>
> **What have you done that you feel proud of? What would you like to be proud of in the future?**
>
> **What qualities do you have that will help you?**

INSPIRING IDEA

Write a letter from your future self with your dream fulfilled. Describe your future self, five or ten years from now, having realised your wishes, hopes and dreams, describing how things are different and how you got there.

Plan a holiday

*We travel, some of us forever, to seek other states,
other lives, other souls. Anaïs Nin*

Most people love to travel. Travel is a great way to experience something new, break away from the everyday and to expand your horizons. Exploring new cultures, foods and languages broadens our understanding of the world and stimulates new interests.

Research has found vacationers and those about to go on holiday are happier than other people. And the more relaxing the holiday, the more lasting the effect. Eventually, though, all holidaymakers return to pre-holiday happiness levels.[47]

Travel appeals to people for different reasons. You may be passionate about the architecture or passionate about the beer. You might like immersing yourself in culture or getting away from it all for solitude and to unwind. You may take a whirlwind trip from site to site or country to country or simply plonk yourself in the one spot and take in the subtleties of daily life.

What gives you itchy feet? Is it a slow crossing of the desert to Varanasi in India, trekking in Nepal, or taking the Trans-Siberian Express Railway through Russia, Mongolia and China? A fast-paced visit to New York or the Carnival in Rio de Janeiro? From the exotic old Moroccan city of Marrakech with its snake charmers, to the Eiffel Tower in Paris, the world is your oyster. Hike to Machu Picchu or be awestruck by the Taj Mahal and the palaces of Rajasthan. Imagine seeing the ballet at the Mariinsky Theatre in

St Petersburg, watching sumo wrestling in Tokyo, or taking tango lessons in Buenos Aires.

You might be after pure relaxation and a space for self-reflection: experience the peacefulness of Buddhist temples in Luang Prabang, Laos; laze on a Thai beach on Koh Phangan island, or soak in Japanese hot springs in Hokkaido.

If you long for nature take a boat trip around Halong Bay in Vietnam; go snorkelling in the Yasawa Islands, Fiji; hike in New Zealand; or gape at the Grand Canyon National Park and Colorado River in Arizona, USA.

Part of the journey is not knowing what you might see, but you're going to see something! And if things don't turn out as expected, sometimes what happens instead is better. Travel teaches us about being flexible, to be open to opportunities and different experiences.

But we don't have to travel halfway around the world to find new experiences: an adventure could be nearby, possibly even close to home. How often have you seen images of places right at home and thought about the beauty of your own country?

Travel can be a good time to reflect and think about life's priorities. In the film *Lost in Translation*, Bob (played by Bill Murray), a fading movie star who travels to Japan to make whiskey commercials, says, 'I'm just completely lost ... I don't know. I just want to ... get healthy. I would like to start taking better care of myself. I'd like to start eating healthier — I don't want all that pasta. I would like to start eating, like, Japanese food.' Like Bob, you might find that a period of reflection away from daily life provides the inspiration you need to make some positive lifestyle changes.

What is your favourite kind of holiday?

What are your top ten travel destinations?

What kinds of things do you do on holiday, where you say to yourself, 'I'd like to continue this when I'm back at home'?

Play with children

Pleasure is very seldom found where it is sought.
Our brightest blazes of gladness are commonly kindled by
unexpected sparks. Samuel Johnson

Playing with your children can be one of the most wonderful things about being a parent. But it's more than just having fun, it's also a vital part of the way babies and children grow and learn. The time you spend having fun together helps your child to learn, to trust and to rely on others. It makes them feel loved and secure and helps them to make sense of the world.

Research tells us that a child's environment and experiences — especially during the first three years of life — strongly influence their development. Play is important for your child's developing self-esteem and social skills; playing with others increases your child's social competence and play helps children to develop an understanding of themselves and their identity.

Children's play ideas can include physically active ball games, using a skipping rope, dancing to music or bike riding. It can also involve quiet time reading or doing arts and crafts. Try collage using old magazines, scissors and glue. Egg cartons and pipe cleaners make spiders, caterpillars and cat's faces with whiskers. Take it outside and paint with sponges, toothbrushes, hands and feet. Explore how colours mix using cellophane or paint. Trace the hands and feet of everyone in the family.

Keep an eye out for useful craft things. Cardboard boxes make excellent cubby houses. Make a pirate's hat out of newspaper. Make play dough from scratch rather than buying it — you only need flour, water, salt and a little food colouring (add a drop or two of essential oil to give your play dough a fun scent). Make musical instruments from glasses filled with water to different heights — tap them with a spoon — or a mini 'guitar' from elastic bands and a lunchbox. Fill jars with rice to make shakers.

Go camping in the backyard, do some gardening together (especially digging and watering), play backyard cricket or football, and let your kids help with washing the car. Go for a walk to the park and listen to the different sounds, blow bubbles, take chalk and draw on the footpath. Have a picnic, play balloon volleyball, or hide and seek.

Singing, storytelling and making shadow puppets can be creative and fun activities. Make a sock puppet with an old sock and two buttons, or dress up in old clothes and make a theatre — let the child decide who will play which role and develop the story together.

Let children take the lead in play. Listen to them and ask questions: 'Wow, that bear is amazing; what's he going to do next?' Of course, you need to make sure the game is safe and doesn't get out of control. Allow plenty of time for experimenting and expect mistakes. Don't compete with young children; this can discourage them from wanting to play with you. Appreciate and encourage your children's effort, tell them you love them and let them know what they did well.

What games do you most enjoy playing with your children?

How have your children made you laugh recently?

If you could increase the time you spend playing with your children or working more, which would you choose?

My commitment to having fun

The things I currently do that are a good way to spend my relaxation and leisure time include:

My goals for improving my relaxation and leisure time are:

What has worked for me in the past is to:

Other sources of support and encouragement I can use are:

I can boost my confidence by:

My next step is to:

PART 3

Keeping on Track

Notice
what's better

The ladder of success is best climbed by stepping on the rungs of opportunity. Ayn Rand

Every now and then, it's helpful to pause and reflect on how things are going. In particular, notice what is better. Think back to how things were when you first opened this book and ask: 'What is better now?'

Scaling can be a useful way to review where you are at and help you visualise the next step towards achieving your goals. Often we have come further on the journey than we had realised.

On a scale from 0 to 10, where 0 is the worst things can be and 10 is how you want things to be, where would you say you are?

What will be different when you get to 1 point higher?

When was the last time you were 1 point higher?

What's the highest you've ever been? What was happening then? How were you able to do that?

What are you doing to stop slipping further down the scale?

If nothing is better: How did you manage to stop things from getting worse?

CREATIVE CHALLENGE

Draw yourself on a journey. Where are you heading? What resources do you need to get you there?

Celebrate your success

Champions aren't made in gyms. Champions are made from something they have deep inside them — a desire, a dream, a vision. They have to have last-minute stamina, they have to be a little faster, they have to have the skill and the will. But the will must be stronger than the skill. Muhammad Ali

Once you've made changes to your life, notice the difference they make. Look at just how far you've come. Take time to make sure you are keeping on track with what is important and meaningful to you. And most importantly, don't forget to celebrate your successes. Like they say, 'Nothing breeds success like success,' so why not celebrate it? From a pat on the back to popping a bottle of champagne, life is too short to not celebrate.

What has improved on your road towards creating more happiness in your life?

What have you been doing to make that happen?

What other things have you noticed? What have others noticed?

How has this made things different for you?

What does that tell you about yourself?

What are your favourite ways to celebrate your success?

Manage setbacks

I have not failed. I've just found 10,000 ways that won't work. Thomas A. Edison

Change is rarely a straightforward process; we go forward, slip back, find our feet, then get re-energised and motivated to have another go. Try to hang in there — allow yourself to take risks and to mess up occasionally. Look for ways to feel more confident about your ability to reach your destination.

Our world is always presenting new opportunities. The great thing about this is that no problem happens all the time or lasts forever. Accept that life has its ups and downs. When things go wrong, you may feel upset, uncertain, even devastated, but only for a short time. Remember this: there are always options.

If you make a slip, think about what has helped you to get back on track in the past. Reflect on the things that have prevented you from slipping further back. What can you learn from this to avoid slips in the future? Consider any other lessons you've learned from these setbacks. Forgive yourself and decide to use the experience as a future resource.

What is getting in the way of you achieving your goals? What could help you to overcome these barriers?

Without the current challenges what would become possible? What would be different?

What are you most looking forward to when the current challenges are gone?

Keep looking for possibilities

We are all in the gutter, but some of us are looking at the stars. Oscar Wilde

Although we all have our habits and ways we like to do things, one thing we can be certain of is that change is constant and inevitable.

Rather than creating big changes, sometimes it's more important to focus on small opportunities when doing something different. Changes are possible with each choice we make. We are continually making decisions to move in one direction or another. Look for clues about what is likely to take you towards more happiness and experiment with doing some of these things.

Problems and solutions are not always directly related — don't go looking for the answer by defining the problem. Rather, describe what the solution will look like. Also, consider the possibility that there may be many different solutions, each of which brings positive change, rather than assuming you need to find only one right solution.

Once you have a rich picture of your goal, practise small steps that are part of the desired outcome: small solutions can lead to big changes. Then make a small yet deliberate positive change: interrupt your usual patterns to explore a path of possibilities towards greater happiness.

Do more of what works. Be open to inviting more happiness into your life. Show up and do your best — nothing else matters.

How do you keep a sense of possibility alive?

What are you getting better at?

How can you sustain the progress you are making?

What new or creative ideas do you have about what could bring extra happiness into your life?

Get help with the jobs you struggle with

It is not so much our friends' help that helps us, as the confidence of their help. Epicurus

When challenges emerge it helps to have a range of resources to draw on. It helps you tackle the problem from different perspectives, and makes success more likely. Friends and family are often great sources of help and support.

There's also a range of professional people who can offer assistance and guidance with resolving whatever problem you face. Doctors, counsellors, financial planners, personal trainers … think about who might help you get on the track to happiness.

Life coaches assist people, organisations or teams to achieve the goal or outcome they want. They work with their client to establish better goals, inspire them to achieve more, empower them with the practical and philosophical tools to do so, motivate them to sustain focus, and steer them towards success. Coaches help people to develop a plan to bridge the gap between where they are now and where they would like to be.

Sometimes, despite our best efforts, we get stuck. We know what we want to be, or do, or create but we need help to get there. Know when to ask for help, and don't feel embarrassed. Offer to help others in return. We can all benefit from the help of others.

Are you accessing the help you need?

What are the key areas of life where some extra help would be useful?

Who could best be of help?

In what ways could they be of help?

What might get in the way of you seeking help? How might you overcome this?

Keep sight
of the big picture

A journey of a thousand miles must begin with a single step. Lao Tzu

Step back and look at the big picture again. I use this tool to regularly check on each of my life domains. I particularly like to do this while on holiday, when I have the space and energy to really pay attention to my life. This exercise helps me to reflect, to check if I'm still on track, to celebrate my successes and to think about where I need to focus my energy. It's a way to assess if I have the balance right and to remember what's important.

Life Domain	What's currently going well	Current goal	Next step
Being your own best friend			
Dressing and grooming			
Designing your living space			
Promoting health and wellbeing			
Managing finances			
Engaging in work			
Building relationships			
Connecting with your community			
Caring for the environment			
Having fun			

Reflect on the change process

*Each problem that I solved became
a rule which served afterwards
to solve other problems.* René Descartes

Consider what has been the most helpful in your change process. What resources did you draw on? What strengths did you use and what mattered most? What commitment can you make to yourself to help sustain the changes you value and want to see continuing in your life?

What have you found useful about this book?

How did the questions enable you to achieve what you have?

What else has been helpful?

Were there times when you were able to keep yourself on track? How did you do that?

What is your next step towards sustaining your efforts?

My commitment to living a happier life

The changes I can celebrate and would like to sustain are:

The fact I have created these changes tells me the following about myself:

I would like to celebrate these changes by:

I am appreciative of the following sources of support and encouragement:

I would like to communicate my appreciation in the following ways:

My next step is to:

My wish for you

You will see wonders. William Shakespeare

I hope you are now walking your path towards greater wellbeing and long-term happiness.

I appreciate the time you have taken to experiment, think, question and challenge yourself. I am wondering whether you've created your own processes to keep yourself motivated and moving towards happiness. What do these say about what you value? I also wonder if you have surprised yourself in what you have been able to achieve.

I wish you a wonderful, fulfilling journey.

May you be well and happy.

Acknowledgements

Many people shared their wisdom and insight, and provided useful reality checks, while I wrote this book. I know that their contributions have helped bring the book alive for readers from different backgrounds, lifestyles and perspectives.

Thank you Rhianon Vichta, Dave Monck, Jill Robards, Penelope Robards, Sekneh Beckett, Melita Smilovic, William Fenton-Smith, Maree Fenton-Smith, Margaret Fenton-Smith, Heidi Fenton-Smith, Nick Radford, Harry Perlich, Trish Corcoran, Adrienne Margarian, Helen Ledingham, Suzie Gibson, David Bennett, Wui Ken Yap, Melissa Kang, Anne Redman, Kareem Tawansi, Claire Grady, Ann Lehmann-Kuit, Alison Winn, Justine Iesu, Karen Weeks, Kristy Lane, Lorrae Carr, Osama Moustafa and John Watson.

Thank you to psychologist Dr Svea van der Hoorn for allowing me to draw on her solution-focused expertise and for reminding me that 'small changes can lead to big improvements'.

Thank you to Siobhan Pope for her sensitive editing, demonstrating the strength of simplicity.

References

1. De Jong, P & Berg, IK 2002, *Interviewing for Solutions*, 2nd edn, Wadsworth, Pacific Grove.

2. Taylor, P, Funk, C & Craighill, P 2010, *Are We Happy Yet?* Washington, DC: Pew Research Center, 2006. [http://www.pewsocialtrends.org/files/2010/10/AreWeHappyYet.pdf]

3. Prochaska, JO & DiClemente, CC 1986, 'Toward a comprehensive model of change', in WR Miller and N Heather (eds.), *Treating addictive behaviors: Processes of change*, Plenum Press, New York, pp. 3–28.

4. Davidhizar, R & Hart, A 2006, 'Are you born a happy person or do you have to make it happen?' *The Health Care Manager*, 25(1), pp. 64–9.

5. Berg, IK & Szabo, P 2005, *Brief Coaching for Lasting Solutions*, WW Norton & Co, New York.

6. Porter, L 1997, *Children are people too: A parent's guide to young children's behaviour,* 2nd edn, Flinders University, Adelaide.

7. Gyatso T [HH The Fourteenth Dalai Lama] 1992, *The Global Community and the Need for Universal Responsibility*, Wisdom Publications, Boston.

8. Eckersley, R 2004, *Well and Good*, Text Publishing, Melbourne.

9. Layard R, Clark A & Senik, C 2012, 'The causes of happiness and misery' in *World Happiness Report*, John Helliwell, Richard Layard and Jeffrey Sachs (eds), The Earth Institute, Columbia University.

10. Headey, B, Muffels, R & Wagner, GG 2010, 'Long-running German panel survey shows that personal and economic choices, not just genes, matter for happiness', *Proceedings of the National Academy of Sciences of the United States of America*, 107(42), pp. 17922–6.

11. World Health Organization 2011, *Obesity and overweight*, http://www.who.int/mediacentre/factsheets/fs311/en/index.html, accessed 7 April 2012.

12. Helliwell, JF, Layard, R & Sachs, J 2012, 'Some policy implications' in *World Happiness Report*, John Helliwell, Richard Layard and Jeffrey Sachs (eds), The Earth Institute, Columbia University.

13. World Health Organization 2012, *Mental Health, Suicide Prevention*, http://www.who.int/mental_health/prevention/suicide/suicideprevent/en/, accessed 7 May 2012.

14. World Health Organization 2009, *Global health risks: Mortality and burden of disease attributable to selected major risks*, http://www.who.int/healthinfo/global_burden_disease/GlobalHealthRisks_report_full.pdf, accessed 29 April 2012.

15. Chida, Y & Steptoe A 2008, 'Positive psychological well-being and mortality: A quantitative review of prospective observational studies', *Psychosomatic Medicine*, 70(7), pp. 741–56.

16. World Health Organization 2004, *Global strategy on diet, physical activity and health*, http://www.who.int/dietphysicalactivity/strategy/eb11344/strategy_english_web.pdf, accessed 25 August 2012.

17. World Health Organization 2010, *Cluster Strategy: Noncommunicable diseases and mental health 2008–2013*, www.who.int/nmh/publications/who_nmh_2009_2/en/index.html, accessed 25 August 2012.

18. Hardy, LL, Denney-Wilson, E, Thrift, AP, Okely, AD & Baur, LA 2010, 'Screen time and metabolic risk factors among adolescents', *Archives of Pediatrics and Adolescent Medicine*, 164(7), pp. 643–9.

19. World Health Organization 2011, *Alcohol factsheet*, www.who.int/mediacentre/factsheets/fs349/en/, accessed 7 April 2012.

20. Rehm, J, 'The risks associated with alcohol use and alcoholism', *Alcohol Research & Health*, 34(2), pp. 135–43.

21. Shaw, M, Mitchell, R & Dorling, D 2000, 'Time for a smoke? One cigarette reduces your life by 11 minutes', *British Medical Journal*, 320(7226), p. 53.

22. Doll, R, Peto, R, Boreham, J & Sutherland, I 2004, 'Mortality in relation to smoking: 50 years' observation on male British doctors', *British Medical Journal*, 328(7455), p. 1519.

23. United Nations, *World Drug Report 2010*, http://www.unodc.org/documents/wdr/WDR_2010/World_Drug_Report_2010_lo-res.pdf, accessed 21 May 2012.

24. Bogduk, N 2004, 'Management of chronic low back pain', *Medical Journal Australia*, 180(2), pp. 79–83.

25. Sachs, J 2012, 'Introduction' in *World Happiness Report*, John Helliwell, Richard Layard & Jeffrey Sachs (eds), The Earth Institute, Columbia University.

26. Easterlin, RA, McVey, LA, Switek, M, Sawangfa, O & Zweig, JS 2010, 'The happiness–income paradox revisited', *Proceedings of the National Academy of Sciences of the United State of America*, 107(52), pp. 22463–8. www.pnas.org/cgi/doi/10.1073/pnas.1015962107

27. Gallup World, http://www.gallup.com/poll/world.aspx, accessed 21 May 2012.

28. Warna, C, Lindholm, L & Eriksson, K 2007, 'Virtue and health — finding meaning and joy in working life', *Scandinavian Journal of Caring Science*, 21(2), pp. 191–8.

29. Mehl, MR, Vazire, S, Holleran, SE & Clark, S 2010, 'Eavesdropping on happiness: Well-being is related to having less small talk and more substantive conversations', *Psychological Science*, 21(4), pp. 539–41.

30. Chapman, G 1992, *Five Love Languages: How to express heartfelt commitment to your mate*, San Val, Missouri.

31. Fowler, JH, Christakis, NA 2008, 'Dynamic spread of happiness in a large social network: Longitudinal analysis over 20 years in the Framingham Heart Study', *British Medical Journal*, 337(a2338).

32. Christakis, NA, Fowler, JH 2007, 'The spread of obesity in a large social network over 32 years', *N Engl JMed*, 357(4), pp. 370–9.

33. Christakis, NA & Fowler JH 2008, 'The collective dynamics of smoking in a large social network', *New England Journal of Medicine*, 358, pp. 2249–58.

34. Rowe, L & Bennett, D 2005, *You can't make me: Seven simple rules for parenting teenagers*, Random House, Sydney.

35. Steptoe, A, O'Donnell, K, Marmot, M & Wardle, J 2008, 'Positive affect and psychosocial processes related to health', *British Journal of Psychology*, 99, pp. 211–27.

36. Davies, JB (ed), *Personal Wealth from a Global Perspective*, UNU-WIDER Studies in Development Economics, Oxford University Press, October 2008.

37. Thoits, PA & Hewitt, LN 2001, 'Volunteer work and well-being', *Journal of Health and Social Behavior*, 42(2), pp. 115–31.

38. United Nations, *Universal Declaration of Human Rights*, http://www.un.org/en/documents/udhr/, accessed 21 May 2012.

39. Samdal, O, Nutbeam, D, Wold, B & Kannas, L 1998, 'Achieving health and educational goals through schools: A study of the importance of the school climate and the students' satisfaction with school', *Health Education Research*, 13(3), pp. 383–97.

40. Natvig, GK, Albrektsen, G & Qvarnstrøm, U 2003, 'Associations between psychosocial factors and happiness among school adolescents', *International Journal of Nursing Practice*, 9(3), pp. 166–75.

41. Berntsson, L, Berg, M, Brydolf, M & Hellstrom, AL 2007, 'Adolescents' experience of well-being when living with a long-term illness or disability', *Scandinavian Journal of Caring Sciences*, 21(4), pp. 419–25.

42. Bruno, MA, Bernheim, JL, Ledoux, D et al. 2011, 'A survey on self-assessed well-being in a cohort of chronic locked-in syndrome patients: Happy majority, miserable minority', *BMJ Open*, 1(1), 1:e000039.

43. Seligman, M 2002, *Authentic Happiness*, Random House, Sydney.

44. Kringelbach, ML & Berridge, KC 2010, 'The neuroscience of happiness and pleasure', *Social Research*, 77(2), pp. 569–678.

45. Cuypers, K, Krokstad, S, Holmen, TL, Knudtsen, MS, Bygren, LO & Holmen, J 2012, 'Patterns of receptive and creative cultural activities and their association with perceived health, anxiety, depression and satisfaction with life among adults: the HUNT study, Norway', *Journal of Epidemiology and Community Health*, 66(8), pp. 698–703.

46. Csikszentmihalyi, M 1991, *Flow: The psychology of optimal experience*, Harper Perennial, San Francisco.

47. Nawijn, J, Marchand, MA, Veenhoven, R & Vingerhoets, AJ 2010, 'Vacationers happier, but most not happier after a holiday', *Applied Research in Quality of Life*, 5(1), pp. 35–47.

Also by Exisle Publishing ...

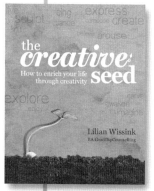

THE CREATIVE SEED

How to enrich your life through creativity

Lilian Wissink BA GradDipCounselling

Creativity is open to us all. Each one of us can discover and nurture a new, exciting dimension in our life!

Whether you are already involved in some form of creative expression, a raw beginner or well established, this book provides a host of strategies to keep you inspired and on track in living your creative dream. Through a combination of case histories, questions and exercises, *The Creative SEED* will:

- *help you to identify the creative interest you would like to explore*
- *enable you to discover your creative strengths*
- *guide you through the creative process using the 'SEED' approach of skills, experimentation, evaluation and discovery, and*
- *help you to overcome common obstacles such as anxiety, stress, low self-confidence and procrastination.*

Whatever your creative pursuit, whether you write, sing, play music, knit, paint or sculpt, turn wood or make pots — *The Creative SEED* will guide you through the everyday ups and downs of the creative process so that you can achieve your goals and more.

ISBN 978 1 921966 25 5

INTUITION

Unlock the power!

Dr Cate Howell

Intuition is something most of us would have experienced at one time or another; it's that gut-feeling or inner voice or 'sixth sense'. It's instinctive by nature, independent of rational analysis or deductive thinking. But can we actively develop our intuition and learn how to better utilise it? Author Dr Cate Howell believes we can, and shows us how in *Intuition*.

In this fascinating book, Dr Howell explores how intuition has been a part of philosophy, psychology, religion and spirituality, from ancient times right up to the present. She also looks at the science behind intuition, and how our experience of it can be described in terms of our brain function. Finally, she sets out a practical seven-step program for developing intuition and using it to enhance everyday life so that we experience an increased sense of peace, purpose and joy.

Practical exercises and meditations are included throughout the book, inviting us to unlock the door to our own intuition garden and encourage it to flourish.

ISBN 978 1 921966 05 7

 **e-newsletter**

If you love books as much as we do, why not subscribe
to our weekly e-newsletter?

As a subscriber, you'll receive special offers and discounts,
be the first to hear of our exciting upcoming titles, and
be kept up to date with book tours and author events.
You will also receive unique opportunities exclusive
to subscribers – and much more!

To subscribe in Australia or from any other
country except New Zealand, visit
www.exislepublishing.com.au/newsletter-sign-up

For New Zealand, visit
www.exislepublishing.co.nz/newsletter-subscribe